DAISY
AND
GOLIATH

Sonia Jones

DAISY AND GOLIATH

EP

Erser & Pond

Cover design by Doug Porter
Cover cartoon by Bruce MacKinnon, reprinted with permission from the Halifax Chronicle Herald

Printed in Canada by Erser & Pond Publishers, Ltd.
1096 Queen St., Suite 225, Halifax, N.S., Canada B3H 2R9
www.erserandpond.com

CANADIAN CATALOGUING IN PUBLICATION DATA
Jones, Sonia
     Daisy and Goliath / Sonia Jones

ISBN   978-0-9781761-2-9

1. Peninsula Farm (N.S.). 2. Jones, Sonia. 3. Yogurt industry—Nova Scotia—Lunenburg (County). 4. Lunenburg (N.S.; County)—Biography. 5. Businesswomen—Nova Scotia—Biography. I. Title.

HD9275.C34P46 2006   338.7'63714760971623   C2006-905928-4

10 9 8 7 6 5 4 3 2

This book is dedicated to my children,
Valerie and Victoria,
to my grandson, Harrison,
and to my identical twin granddaughters,
Alexa and Danica.
May they live long, happy, and productive lives
under the protective wing
of a just and loving government.

Harrison (8 yrs) holds Alexa (left) and
Danica (5 months old)

Contents

Acknowledgments

No company can succeed, or even fail gracefully, without a team effort. It is with the deepest gratitude, therefore, that I mention here two of the key players who remained loyal to the very end (even if they were not necessarily on the payroll at the time of closure): Sylvia Booth (office manager), and Blair Landry (plant manager). Their hard-working assistants were Crystal Berringer (accounts payable), Cheryl Lohnes (accounts receivable), Jim Cooper (computer programming), Rick Joudrey (fleet maintenance), Craig Schrader (plant maintenance), Michelle Jackson (production), and Janet Robertson (sales). The stores were overseen by Norman Gallant (merchandising supervisor) and his enormous crew of assistants who are too numerous to mention, except to say that they all deserve medals for not allowing themselves to be deterred by rain, snow, sleet, or hail in their effort to make sure that the yogurt was always on the store shelves and nicely displayed for the enjoyment of the consumers. As a matter of fact, all our employees deserve medals for going far beyond the call of duty in making sure that the yogurt was produced on time, and that the product was always pure and safe.

And that brings us to the customers. Hats off to our many loyal customers who bought Peninsula Farm yogurt in spite of heavy competition from the multi-national dairy conglomerates that were forever offering two-for-one sales, cents-off coupons, deep discounts, and other forms of irresistible temptation. Our yogurt, on the other hand, was never on sale. The price was based on the cost of labor and ingredients – it was as simple as that. But our customers, people of obviously discerning taste, continued to be faithful to our brand. For this we shall always be deeply grateful.

We are also indebted to the government of Canada for the many awards we were given over the years for entrepreneurship and product development. We are somewhat less grateful to the public servants who deemed it necessary to put an end to a company that was carefully built stone by stone, so to speak, with enormous hard work dedication. But of course, they were only doing their jobs.

Sonia Jones

Sonia Jones
Chief Executive Officer
Peninsula Farm Limited

Prologue

Peninsula Farm, the yogourt manufacturing business in Lunenburg, Nova Scotia, was once a small business success story and a cultural icon in the province. Many people thought it was such an interesting and uplifting story that someone should write a book about it, so my wife, Sonia Jones, rolled up her sleeves and went to work. Her book was called *It All Began With Daisy,* and it was published in 1987 by E.P. Dutton, a division of Penguin Books in New York. It was condensed by the *Reader's Digest,* published in over a dozen languages, and adopted by the *Literary Guild of America.* Some movie deals were bandied about, but the story never went into production.

As the proud husband and business partner of the author, I was asked to write the prologue to this book, so I decided to prepare myself for the task by reading the foreword that I wrote twenty years ago for *It All Began With Daisy.* I found the last paragraph, written while we were vacationing in Hawaii, to be instructive, although it leaves a lot of questions unanswered: *Success is ephemeral, and there's never any guarantee that it'll last forever. I don't know what the future holds for Peninsula Farm. Will our giant competitors find a way to put us down? Will our chain-store customers "deal" us out of the market-place? Will the distributing dairies buy our shelf space? Or will we become an international conglomerate, licensing dairies all over the world to make our products? What I do know is that we will start the New Year as we finished the old – interested only in making the best yogurt, fighting always to be a successful business, and preserving our quality no matter what the cost.*

Since Peninsula Farm closed, we've been asked hundreds of times to explain what happened. People thought it was such an infuriating and outrageous story that someone should write a book about it, so once again my wife rolled up her sleeves and went to work on the sequel. The answers to the questions I asked myself in Hawaii are contained herein. Without giving away the story, I think it's instructive to say that Sonia decided to call it *Daisy and Goliath*. If you had asked me in Hawaii who the future Goliath would be, I would have assumed he would be the multinational conglomerates that were looming large over the horizon of the business landscape. I was not far from wrong. What I didn't realize at the time, however, was the extent to which big business would go hand in hand with the self-interest of big government. Sonia's story of our continued adventures and misadventures incisively captures the nuances of the business world of the new millennium.

Gordon Jones

Gordon Jones, President
Peninsula Farm Limited

CHAPTER ONE

Apocalypse

In the main office at Peninsula Farm is a framed certificate that reads, *"Canada Award for Business Excellence, granted by the Government of Canada to Sonia Jones (President) and Gordon Jones (Treasurer) in recognition of the exceptional contribution of Peninsula Farm Limited to the Province of Nova Scotia and its business community."*

Next to it on the wall is a framed picture of a Canadian flag overlaid with the following words written, once again, by federal agents of the government of Canada: *"Join Team Canada. Jump start the Canadian economy. Give work to Canadian companies. By doing the work in Canada by Canadians you support our school systems, hospitals, and local communities. Assure yourself top Canadian quality and expertise."*

The view from cow heaven

The small dairy plant opposite our farmhouse looks dreary and defeated. It crouches behind tractor-trailers, stacks of wooden pallets, and an assortment of empty cream cans. Two stainless steel milk storage tanks stand forlornly under scudding clouds, awaiting a milk delivery that will never come. There is a gaping hole in the plant wall through which stainless steel vats and filling machines have been dragged out, loaded onto flatbeds, and driven away. The tiled floor inside the factory is chipped and scored by the heavy moving equipment. Gordon and I stand there, numbed by shock, surveying the devastation.

To the average onlooker there is nothing surprising about this disheartening scene. No little pint-sized yogurt factory can expect to survive in today's competitive world of free trade and rampant globalization. An intelligent observer would naturally conclude that the company had been forced to close its doors as a result of heavy competition from the multinational conglomerates that have invaded the Maritime Provinces in recent years. Why would the local supermarket chains want to make room for a small family business when the global corporations can pull such sweet deals from their deep pockets? And why would consumers want to pay a little bit more for local products when the food industry giants can undercut them so easily?

Gordon and I once thought we had the answers. The motto we devised for our company during the early years was, *"If you have to be the smallest, then you'd better be the best."* We were convinced that it was the fundamental reason for our success. Under normal circumstances we would have been right – we all know what happens when a better mousetrap hits the market. But when we wrote our company motto we didn't foresee that the world would be radically changed by the powerful forces of globalization. It would be a world where prices are dictated by multinational giants, where consumer choices are restricted by corporate interests, where work is outsourced around the globe, and where family farms and small enterprises are routinely demolished by a barrage of foreign imports.

How it all began

But when my husband and I moved to Nova Scotia in 1972, we were living in a world of unlimited possibilities. Gordon was born and raised in Brooklyn, where there is so little greenery that a whole book was written about a tree that once grew there. Who could have guessed that he would end up being a dairy farmer in rural Nova Scotia? Moreover, if

anyone had ever told me I was destined to be the Yogurt
Queen of Eastern Canada within 15 years of earning a PhD
in Romance Languages from Harvard University, I'd have
had him committed.

Yet life abounds in unfathomable ironies, so naturally
that's exactly what happened. Gordon and I became the
baffled owners of a very small yogurt manufacturing
company that competed successfully with international
players such as Beatrice, Kraft, Sealtest, Yoplait, and
Parmalat (under the Astro label) – all because we bought a
Jersey cow in an unguarded moment.

For those of you who have not read *It All Began with Daisy,*
it behooves you to know that our story began in Manhattan,
where my husband owned a thriving management consulting
business on Park Avenue. When my newly minted doctorate
failed to land me a professorship in the New York area,
Gordon saw this as an opportunity to escape the boredom of
his daily routine and throw himself into the arms of an
uncertain future.

"Look for a job anywhere you want," he urged me.
"Just make sure it's somewhere near the ocean."

Gordon was an avid yachtsman and was fed up with the
traffic jams on Long Island Sound, so when I received an
offer to teach at Dalhousie University in Halifax, Nova
Scotia, I eagerly accepted.

One thing soon led to another. The oceanfront property
we bought just happened to be a farm, and before we knew it
our good neighbor was prevailing upon us to get some
"critters" to "gnaw off the grass" so it wouldn't revert back
to alder bush. The last thing we wanted to do was ruin the
land that the local farmers had tended for generations, so we
dutifully drove our truck to an auction and purchased the
necessary beef cattle. It also seemed like an eminently

sensible idea to get a cow as well, for all of us, including baby Valerie, were inordinately fond of dairy products.

Daisy quickly made herself the head of the household, subordinating us to the position of lackeys in charge of cleaning, feeding, and milking her. We meekly accepted our servitude, for which Daisy rewarded us by producing more milk than we knew what to do with. We tried reasoning with her, but she seemed unwilling to cut back her milk supply, nor did she understand anything about Sundays and holidays. When the provincial dairy commission informed us that we were not allowed to sell our milk to the local creamery for at least nine months (until quota could be allotted to us for that purpose), we decided to make the surplus milk into yogurt for a nearby health food store.

I spent endless days and nights trying to incubate milk in the oven, in the furnace room, and even in a heat-controlled tropical fish tank, but I was so unsuccessful that Gordon had to go out and buy a herd of pigs to eat my mistakes. This was an enormous comfort to me, as the pigs turned out to be uncritical admirers of all my abortive efforts.

After much trial and many errors I eventually settled on a system using Styrofoam picnic boxes that doubled as delivery cases. As for perfecting the recipe itself, it seemed a simple task to put out a premium yogurt using fresh milk, frozen fruit, and no preservatives or artificial ingredients. The truth is, of course, that I wouldn't have known where to locate preservatives or even "all natural" additives even if I had wanted to use them.

The results were frankly irresistible. I remember vaguely wondering why other dairies didn't produce a similar item.

Apparently there were a good number of discriminating consumers who agreed that Daisy's yogurt was indeed a special treat, for soon orders began flowing in from other health food stores as well as delicatessens and various independent outlets. As word spread and sales increased, the white Styrofoam boxes multiplied until they lined all the walls of the first floor of our house. Our little girls grew up thinking that a normal dwelling in the province of Nova Scotia was something akin to an igloo made of Styrofoam.

By this time we had begun to realize that we had been sucked down the yogurt trail by a sort of invisible vacuum cleaner. There was nothing for us to do but lie back and enjoy the ride. After three years we were making about $50,000 a year in our kitchen. Visitors came swarming to the farm in search of the homemade ice cream I had learned to make with Daisy's surplus cream. But the cramped conditions in our house made it abundantly clear to us that we would soon have to construct a yogurt factory to handle the constantly growing demand.

A real education

Gordon, who used to while away his days in New York advising his corporate clients on the finer points of venture capitalism, was delighted to be head over heels in debt. But I was not used to the realities of business, and I promptly panicked. I wanted to amortize the cost of our shiny new factory as quickly as possible, so while Gordon milked the cows I went forth into the world in search of new accounts.

And so it was that my real education began, ten years after earning my PhD. I soon learned that a manufacturer hoping to place a product in the chain stores must pay for the listing and the shelf space, as well as provide rebates, volume discounts, and co-op advertising fees. To do this I was advised by the chain store buyers that I would have to cut costs by making yogurt with powdered milk instead of fresh milk, and using a fruit-like industrial "preparation" instead of cooking my own fresh frozen berries. I would also be in a better position to pay rebates, they assured me, if I reduced the amount of fruit by half and added artificial flavor or "natural" flavor enhancers. It would also be more profitable for me, I was told, if I included some preservatives to increase the shelf life, since I was automatically expected to replace any yogurt that didn't sell by the expiry date or that was spoiled because of faulty refrigeration in the store. If I didn't "adapt" to these realities, I could never hope to succeed in the highly competitive yogurt market.

Gordon and I decided not to adapt. We refused to compromise the quality of our yogurt, making do instead with the worst and least shelf space available. We visited all the stores to make sure that what little space we had was well stocked, and we carefully rotated the containers so the oldest ones were in the front. We devised a complex inventory control system to keep our credits to a minimum, and we ensured the freshness of the product by pulling it from the shelves five days before the expiry date.

Yet in spite of all our efforts, our sales were not what we expected. The chain store customers were far less interested in yogurt than the health food enthusiasts had been, so Gordon decided to set up a booth in a different store each week and hand out free samples. It was an uphill battle all the way, for in those days many people saw yogurt as a rather exotic food compared to their usual fare. But Gordon persevered. By dint of tenacity, humor, and irrepressible energy, he managed to persuade even the most reluctant shoppers to give our product a try, until eventually it became known as "the yogurt that even yogurt-haters love."

It was a laborious and frustrating way to penetrate the market, but it worked in the long run. Although word-of-mouth proceeds at a rather leisurely pace, we believed it was actually the best form of advertising, and the price was certainly right. Perhaps the most important result of our slow progress in the early years is that it prevented us from going off the deep end financially. We allowed the market to dictate our rate of growth, so we were able to maintain a healthy cash flow and a fairly well balanced debt/equity ratio.

If it was naiveté that initially spurred us into playing David to the Goliath food industry, it was obstinacy, hard work, careful startup cost management, and above all a premium quality product that permitted us to succeed. We proved that successful industries could be developed in rural areas where the lifestyle may provide an attractive alternative to some of the grimmer realities of urban living. We also showed that small can indeed be beautiful, and that it may, in fact, be the only way to ensure the survival of top quality products in the marketplace.

Looking back on it all today, I realize that it was this same naiveté that helped us to march blindly forward in those early years. I had no idea what I was getting myself into. I'm sure that if I had had the slightest inkling of what it was like to deal with unnecessary delays, colossal batch failures, terrifying price wars, equipment breakdowns, supply shortfalls, profit-killing rebate demands, conniving competitors, arrogant food buyers, employee error, and Napoleonic dairy case boys, I would never have had the temerity to take on the dairy industry.

But sometimes it's a good thing not to know too much. Fortunately for me I wasn't aware that it was impossible for a housewife to transfer her homemade yogurt recipes to the store shelves, or for a lowly Spanish professor to balance a dairy business on her mortarboard. Nor did Gordon seem to notice, for that matter, that the streets of Brooklyn were not the ideal training ground for milking cows and mucking out barns. We just kept muddling along on a day-to-day basis, meeting all the new emergencies as they arose. "Vigorous muddling," we called it.

While we never developed the fondness for crises that marks the true entrepreneur, we became well acquainted with disaster and learned to face most catastrophes with a certain equanimity. We readily admit that we lost all sorts of time and money by learning the dairy business through trial and error, and we were informed more than once by the "experts" that we were crazy to reinvent the wheel when good advice could have been provided by the consulting sector.

But insanity has its advantages. We had absolutely no preconceived notions about how yogurt "must" be made in the industry today, or what formulas and procedures to follow in developing a product that would enjoy consumer "acceptance." All we had to go by were our taste buds and a certain modicum of common sense. When an experiment succeeded, my family let me know. When it didn't work out to my satisfaction, I donated it to the pigs and tried again. I did not, however, encourage my porcine friends to join any of our taste test panels, as they had a disconcerting tendency to greet even my worst efforts with squeals of unbridled enthusiasm.

The end result of my frustrating experiments was the development of a yogurt that was thought to be unique in the dairy industry. In spite of the fact that there was supposed to be no such thing as homemade yogurt on the supermarket shelves, ours was nevertheless very real and going strong.

When people asked why Peninsula Farm yogurt was so highly esteemed by connoisseurs, I could only say that it was because we decided early on to take the road less traveled. In order to translate my original kitchen recipes to a large-scale operation, I had to do things the hard way. It meant spending a bit of extra money on labor and ingredients, and it certainly meant that more time and effort had to be devoted to carrying out some pretty unusual procedures.

But who in his right mind, you ask, would want to do things the hard way?

Nobody, of course, unless she just happens to be a naïve Spanish professor married to a quixotic farmer from deep in the heart of Brooklyn.

CHAPTER TWO

Gathering Clouds

The handwriting on the wall

The phones at Peninsula Farm were ringing non-stop. Our merchandisers in Nova Scotia, New Brunswick, and Prince Edward Island were calling to report that the shelf space allocated to our yogurt had been drastically reduced in the two supermarket chains that dominate the market in the Maritime Provinces. When our shelf stockers arrived at the stores that morning they thought our product had been delisted. But when they looked more closely they found a small number of yogurt containers sitting mournfully in the top left-hand corner of the dairy cases, almost out of sight and certainly out of reach to anyone but the tallest customers with the longest arms and the strongest fingers.

"This is awful," groaned Janet, our head merchandiser in New Brunswick. "They've taken away half our shelf space, and they never even told us they were going to do it!"

Manufacturers of perishable products in the food industry are required by the supermarket chains to send their own shelf stockers (or "merchandisers") on a regular basis to the stores to move the products from the back coolers to their assigned positions on the shelves. Most dairy suppliers can easily afford to provide this service since they handle large quantities of fresh milk and a variety of other products, making their store visits financially worthwhile. But in our case it's extremely costly to hire merchandisers, paying them mileage and an hourly wage to go to all the stores for the sole purpose of moving our yogurt from the back coolers onto the dairy case shelves. It would be much more efficient to have store employees stock the dairy cases, but it saves the supermarkets time and money to have this service provided by the suppliers.

"Let's take it one step at a time," I said to Janet, trying to stay calm in the face of our latest crisis. "First of all, where is the yogurt that was removed from the shelves?"

"It's all in the back coolers, but it's in terrible shape. They tossed our containers into plastic milk crates. Some of them broke, and yogurt spilled all over the containers underneath."

"Who took our product off the shelves?" I asked.

"Baxter's Dairy did the re-line. They're distributing a new yogurt called Astro."

I knew about Astro. It was once a family company owned by two brothers from Eastern Europe who ran a delicatessen in Toronto. When the going got tough they sold the firm to a couple of entrepreneurs who then turned around and re-sold it to a transnational conglomerate by the name of Parmalat, located in Parma, Italy, a region famous for its Parmesan cheese. Astro yogurt, once pure and natural when it was produced by the original family, had now gone the way of all flesh.

"So then it was Baxter's that smashed up our yogurt?"

"Gotta be," said Janet. "They were the ones who rearranged the dairy cases. And our yogurt is in their milk crates, so who else could it be?"

Who indeed? Was there a note of triumphalism or a touch of hostility in the way our competitors treated our yogurt? Perhaps it was only carelessness on the part of the

Baxter's merchandisers in handling a product for which they bore no responsibility. Why bother to take reasonable care of our yogurt when they were being paid to put another company's product in its place?

Baxter's Dairy, once a locally-owned business in Saint John, New Brunswick, had at that time been purchased by a huge cooperative in British Columbia called Dairyland, and they were looking for coast-to-coast representation. Like other large companies that buy out small businesses, Dairyland chose to operate under the Baxter logo in this region. If nothing else, it gave the public the impression that they were local players.

"The receivers have refused to accept our deliveries today," Janet went on. "They say there's not enough room in the back coolers for extra stock, so they told the drivers to take it away. All six of our tractor/trailers are returning to the plant in Lunenburg fully loaded with a whole week's supply of yogurt. What are we going to do with all that extra stock?"

I groaned inwardly. Why couldn't the stores have done us the courtesy of warning us that they were cutting our shelf space in half to make room for Astro yogurt? What was so difficult about picking up the phone and letting us know their plans so we could cut back our production accordingly? Now we would lose a week's sales, warehousing stock that would lose a week's worth of shelf life.

But the worst of it was that we would lose half our sales every week forever after. Obviously the decision-makers at the head offices of the supermarket chains didn't relish the idea of having to listen to me complain about the effect this would have on our company. They had heard all my arguments before, and had become adept at turning a deaf ear to my concerns. Why should they waste their time considering my plight when the multinationals were offering them deals that could never be matched by a small family business?

"And that's not all," Janet continued. "The stores are demanding credit for all the yogurt that was removed from the shelves. They want us to take it away, too, along with the product we were trying to deliver this morning. They're making us pay for the damaged yogurt, too."

Why was I not surprised? It is the policy of all stores that products be shipped to them on a "guaranteed" basis. This means that the supplier is responsible for anything that might happen to the product before it is purchased by the consumer. If the refrigeration in the store breaks down for any reason, the supplier or manufacturer must give the store credit for the damaged product. If the "code date" (otherwise known as the "best before date") on a product expires, the manufacturer must give the store its money back. If a customer drops a product and damages it the manufacturer is required to pay, while smiling store employees gladly accept the customer's gratitude for what appears to be their unquestioning generosity. If product is damaged in the back storage cooler by competitors who are a little rough in their handling of pallet jacks, once again it is the manufacturer's responsibility to credit the store for the product. In other words, all risks are assumed by the supplier and none by the stores.

"Don't worry, Janet," I said. "I'll call the guys at head office and see what I can do to persuade them to give us back at least some of our shelf space."

I couldn't tell Janet I had already seen the handwriting on the wall, forged in large, menacing letters by the anonymous rulers of the new global economy that moves ineluctably forward, putting small local businesses into a state of constant panic. Nothing good could come of my threatening the company morale at this point. Besides, I wasn't yet prepared to ask myself for whom the bells were tolling. I was in a fighting mood.

The bottom line

The first call I made was to the head office of the Sobeys supermarket chain in Stellarton, Nova Scotia. Of the two chains that still remained in the Maritime Provinces, Sobeys was the locally-owned company. The other one, Atlantic Wholesalers, had been purchased by Loblaw's, a large national corporation with its headquarters in Toronto. Loblaw's also acquired the Maritime IGAs, some corner stores, and the Capitol stores (later renamed "Fresh Marts" and then "Needs"). Since it was well known to Maritimers that Sobeys was a local company, Loblaw's decided to name its largest outlets "Real Atlantic Superstores," in the hope that they, too, would be thought to be locally owned. It's all in the perception.

The category manager for dairy products at the Sobeys head office was polite but firm as he explained to me that the new planogram describing the current space allocations in the dairy cases had, essentially, been written in stone. It was impossible to change this planogram by even so much as one facing (a "facing" refers to the amount of space needed to stock one row of containers all the way to the back of the shelf).

"We try to be fair to everyone," the category manager said. "We only have so much space in the dairy cases, so we had to cut all the yogurt suppliers back to make room for Astro. Nobody's happy about this, take my word for it. I've been getting complaints all week."

He sounded tired. Everybody has problems.

"Yes, but when you take eight feet away from Danone, it's only a tenth of their overall space on the shelves. But when you take eight feet away from us, it amounts to half of our space overall."

"I know what you're saying," he sighed, with admirable patience. But we've based our decisions on market share.

Your sales are down, so your new space reflects that fact. There's not much I can do about it, I'm afraid."

There was no denying that our market share had been slipping steadily for the past few years. In its heyday Peninsula Farm enjoyed the lion's share of the market in the Maritime Provinces, holding its own against such behemoths as Yoplait and Beatrice, as well as a national dairy called Delisle and a local dairy known as Farmer's Cooperative Dairy. Farmer's, the smallest of our competitors, was only 100 times larger than we were. But Delisle (a dairy based in Quebec) was 1,000 times our size, while Beatrice (an American company) was many thousands of times our size, and Yoplait (a multinational conglomerate with headquarters in France) was at least 15,000 times larger than we were.

"According to the information we received from the Neilsen survey," the category manager at Sobeys continued, "your market share has dropped to 7%."

"But Neilsen's doesn't take into account the fact that we're not in all the stores," I explained. "If you compared our sales sku for sku (pronounced "skew," for "stock-keeping unit") with our competition in the stores where we *do* sell our yogurt, you'd find that our market share is much better than that."

"Nevertheless, your sales are down. What can I say? It's just one of those things."

"But which came first, the chicken or the egg? Our sales go down because we keep losing shelf space every time you decide to hand it over to our competitors. So naturally the decrease in our sales becomes a self-fulfilling prophecy."

Although the category manager continued to make mildly sympathetic noises, he was not about to give us back our shelf space.

The same thing had happened when Danone came on the scene (a French company with annual sales of over twenty billion dollars). Our space had been cut back drastically when a deal was struck with that powerful conglomerate, and the big chain stores were not willing to alter their lucrative arrangement just because a little family-owned local business was facing a serious crisis as a result of that decision. The transnationals have deeper pockets than most of us can imagine.

"You have to try to understand that we owe it to our customers to provide them with variety," said the category manager, almost apologetically. "Choice is everything."

"But the problem is that the mass-produced yogurts are all pretty much the same," I said. "They're on a par with ordinary table wine. The average person would be hard-pressed to tell the difference. But here I am, offering you the Châteauneuf-du-Pape of yogurts, and you're squeezing me out!"

"What kind of yogurt was that, did you say?"

"The best yogurt. I'm offering you the best yogurt that money can buy. That's an important part of the customer choice that you were referring to earlier."

The category manager said nothing. We both knew that in the end it's not about excellence. It's about the bottom line.

Am I losing my marbles?

When I put down the receiver I called the Sobeys head office again and asked to speak to David Sobey himself. He had long ago asked me to contact him if I ran into any major problems, but I hadn't wanted to trouble him with every little snag I encountered as I struggled along in the shadow of the towering yogurt giants. I was fortunate, however, in that Sobey saw himself as a godfather to our little company. His wife, Faye, had come across our product many years before in a Halifax health food store and had liked it so much that she had had prevailed upon her husband to list it in his outlets all across Nova Scotia.

"We could never do that, we only have one cow!" I had exclaimed, as he stood in our kitchen contemplating our very limited production facilities.

"Don't be too quick to say no," Sobey had said. "After all, my grandfather started out with just one store. Why don't you get yourself a second cow and make some yogurt for one of my stores? When you can see your way clear to getting a third cow, I'll call the manager of the second store and tell him you're coming. Then when you're ready for the fourth cow, I'll call the third store, and so on. You'll be able to grow at your own pace. What do you say?"

"It's a deal," said Gordon, knowing a good thing when he heard it. And from that moment on we were in the yogurt business. There was no end in sight.

As soon as Atlantic Wholesalers (a locally-owned company back in those days) realized that Sobeys was carrying a natural, home-made yogurt that was becoming popular, their president, Al Rose, came to the farm and asked us to make some yogurt for his company, too. It wasn't long before Norman Newman, the owner of the Capitol Stores, also paid us a visit. Soon we were receiving calls from various health food stores and independent outlets, all wanting to buy the yogurt that was fast becoming the talk of the town.

A deep voice on the other end of the line interrupted my nostalgic dreams.

"Sonia? This is David Sobey. My assistant tells me you're having some problems. They've cut back your shelf space, have they?"

"Yes, they've given half of it to Astro. Do you think there's any way I could get at least some of it back?"

"There's not much I can do on my end, I'm afraid. I've talked to my people and they tell me they made a solid, written deal with Astro. They can't exactly go and change the terms and conditions after the fact."

"This may put us out of business, you know."

"I'm sorry to hear that. I really am. We go back a long way. How many years has it been? Close to thirty, it seems to me. Gordon must be about ready to retire, isn't he?"

"Yes, but how can we retire if we lose the business? We'll end up with nothing, and neither of us has a pension."

"You taught for many years at Dalhousie, didn't you?"

"Yes, but I was too young to qualify for a retirement pension when I left."

"Well, you must have plenty of equity in Peninsula Farm, don't you?"

"But what good is equity if we don't have a business to sell? Nobody in his right mind would want to be in our shoes now, with the transnational conglomerates breathing down our necks. Who would ever buy us?"

"Maybe one of the large dairies will make you an offer."

"I don't think so. Why would they bother? It's cheaper for them to just slowly absorb all our shelf space. Anyway, even if I had a million dollars to make you a better deal on the space, I'd lose out to the fellow who has ten or twenty million to throw around. The cost of doing business has gone right off the charts. The guy with the most marbles ends up winning."

"Globalization seems to have become a fact of life these days, hasn't it?" Sobey remarked sorrowfully. "These are hard times for small enterprises. I'm sorry it turned out this way for you. Let me know if there's anything I can do."

"It looks as though a whole generation of progress is going to be erased with one sweep of the hand!" I said. "It's sad."

"I'm sorry."

"So where do we go from here? Do you think one gigantic world conglomerate will end up owning everything some day?"

"I guess I'll never know. I don't think I'll be around to see it happen."

I was sure I detected a hint of relief in his voice.

Immoral woman on the loose!

There was nothing for it but to give Atlantic Wholesalers a call, but I wasn't holding my breath. If David Sobey, a Maritimer familiar with the problems of the local economy, was not prepared to give us back our shelf space, then the Toronto-based "Atlantic" Wholesalers Corporation would not be of much help to us, either.

My conversation with the category manager for dairy products at Atlantic Wholesalers' head office quickly confirmed my suspicions.

"We can't give you back your space," he said. "Your sales aren't there. How could I justify that?"

"My sales are down because you took away my space," I said wearily. How often would I have to explain that?

"Why don't you look closer at what your competition is doing?" he suggested. "You should put your yogurt in those little multipacks, like the others are doing. People love those multipacks. They stick them in their lunch boxes. You should do something like that."

"Do you know how much a multipack filling machine costs? Over a million dollars! The machine forms the plastic cups at the same time it fills them."

"Well, have you seen the tubes that Yoplait is putting out? Now *there's* an idea for you. Kids are wild about them. They squeeze the stuff out of the tubes like toothpaste. Why don't you go for something like that? You've gotta keep up with the Joneses, right?"

"I can't afford a filling machine that does tubes, either!"

"What can I tell you? You'll have to be creative if you want to survive. Why don't you put some bright colors in your product? Kids love bright colors."

"We don't do bright colors. We do all natural." I was mortified by how self-righteous I sounded just then.

"Well, there aren't enough people who care about all natural to keep you going, believe me. Sock the color to it, that's what I say. Put some dinosaurs on the packaging. Get with the program. But hey, I'm not trying to tell you what to do. It's your business. Do what you like."

I decided to try to get in touch with a higher authority at Atlantic Wholesalers. Not that I had any hope of persuading them to reverse their decision, but I didn't want to leave any stones unturned. After punching my way through countless menus and listening to more than my fair share of musack, I finally got an executive officer on the phone. I described the crisis we were facing and explained that we would probably go out of business if we couldn't get our sales back to where they had been before our space was cut back. I was not prepared for his response.

"It's downright immoral of you to talk to me about going out of business."

I didn't think I heard him right.

"What? What's immoral about it?"

"You think you can get special treatment if you give me a sob story about being a local business that's about to go belly up. Well, it's not going to work."

"You're calling me *immoral?*"

"Look, I don't have time for this."

"I'm just trying to point out what's going on in the business world today. It's not good for either of us. If small businesses in Nova Scotia keep getting squeezed out by the transnational conglomerates there'll be fewer and fewer local businesses, and then you won't have as many customers, either. People will have to look for jobs in France or Italy, and I'll bet the owners of Yoplait and Danone and Astro aren't going to be just standing there waiting for them to arrive at the factory door."

There was a whooshing sound from the other end of the line. I thought the executive officer had sneezed, but it turned out to be a snort of disdain.

"You needn't be concerned about our customers, Mrs. Jones. We have plenty of them, thank you very much."

"But I'm sure you know that most jobs here are created by locally-owned businesses," I persisted. "If they go down, it's bound to affect employment."

I paused to give him a chance to respond, but there was no answer.

"There won't be any work for local cows, either," I added, hoping to defrost him with a lighter touch. "Nova Scotia really *will* end up being Canada's ocean playground, just as it says on the license plates."

"The small businesses around here are doing just fine," he replied, with perfect self-assurance. "In my experience people go out of business because of poor management. So don't be a victim. Take responsibility. Don't try to blame it on shelf space."

"Poor management? It takes *excellent* management to stay in business for 25 years when all your competitors are corporations that are 20,000 times your size! Besides, if shelf space isn't important, why does everyone pay so much for it?"

"Let me make something perfectly clear, Mrs. Jones. We do *not* sell shelf space. And let me tell you something else. You're lucky to be in our stores. And we're not under any obligation to keep you in them, either."

There was a click on the other end of the line.

My heart was thumping. What was his *problem?* I had clearly touched a nerve when I mentioned selling shelf space, but I knew for certain that people were paying big bucks for *something,* however he wanted to describe it.

CHAPTER THREE

When Editors Hanker for Ice-Cream

Judging the book by its cover

Gordon laughed when I got home that night and told him about my somewhat surrealistic conversation with the executive from Atlantic Wholesalers.

"So my wife is an immoral woman, is she? What a hoot! Don't spread it around. The guys in Lunenburg would have a lot of fun with that. I'd never hear the end of it."

"Gordon, be serious," I said, wanting to get him focused on our shelf space problems. I was still seething about the way we'd been treated. "What really bugs me is that we've been paying rebates to Atlantic Wholesalers ever since we started the business. Maybe we didn't pay as much as the other suppliers, but it was all we could afford. We never took any profit for ourselves – it all went into rebates. And what did that do for us? We'd have been better off paying them nothing at all."

"Then they would have had the perfect excuse to throw us out altogether," Gordon said, leaning back in his chair.

"But they'd have lost a good customer, too. Do you realize how much fruit we've bought from them over the years? And where did *that* get us? Nobody remembers the pallet loads of fruit."

"The people we used to deal with in the old days would remember. There was a family atmosphere here in Nova Scotia back then. We were all doing business on a level playing field, and we treated each other right. But now they're sending their boys here from Toronto to teach us how immoral we are. We've come to the end of an era."

"I wish there were some way to get out of this gracefully, without losing the whole shooting match. What can we do to save the company?"

"It's up to the consumers, I guess. The supermarkets are trying to tell them what to put in their shopping carts by controlling what goes onto the shelves, but the customers don't *have* to buy any of the products they don't want and don't like. Nobody can force people to buy iridescent yogurt in toothpaste tubes. If everyone insists on buying the best products regardless of the packaging, we'll be okay."

"But there are still a lot of people out there who tend to judge a book by its cover. How can we get it across to them that Peninsula Farm is something different? We don't have money to advertise, we don't have money to sweeten any deals, and we certainly can't afford to produce yogurt in every size, shape, and flavor.

"Making great yogurt is no small thing," Gordon said. "We've always claimed that if you have to be the smallest, then you'd better be the best."

"But how can we get this across to the public if we have no money? A whole new generation of people has been born since we started our business, and most of them don't know anything about us. They probably don't even know we're the only local company left with a yogurt brand name."

"I think it's time for you to write the sequel to *It All Began with Daisy*. Just tell it like it is. People recognize the truth when they hear it."

I stared at him. "We're right in the middle of a crisis here, and you want me to sit down and write another *book?*"

"What else can you do? You've got to take over the reins. You need to tell our story. We're not the only small business that's being threatened by globalization. Maybe your book will help pull us all together. We can't just wring our hands and let the transnationals call the shots. We'll have to come up with some creative solutions of our own."

"But I don't have the answers."

"Don't worry about that. The first thing to do is clarify the questions. Just write it down the way it happened. Small business owners everywhere will recognize themselves in your story. Make your book a clarion call for justice. Show some leadership. Inform the populace. Rally the troops. The multinational conglomerates may have the sword right now, but you have the pen. So use it!"

An avalanche of rejection slips

Write another book? Was this a case of déjà vu? Gordon's request that I write a sequel to our story put me in mind of a wintry Saturday morning ten years after we had been lured into the confusing and perilous quagmire known as the dairy industry. Gordon had leaned close to me as I prepared my classes for my students at Dalhousie University. I thought he was going to whisper a few little sweet nothings in my ear.

"I've lost my voice," he croaked, his breath warming my skin. "I've done so many demos that I've gone hoarse."

A *demo* refers to the "demonstration" of the merits of a product through the provision of free samples to unwary shoppers who happen to push their carts past the supplier's demo booth. Gordon had "demoed" our yogurt for three days a week for a whole year in each one of the stores we serviced, which caused our sales to increase their volume in direct proportion to the decrease in volume of Gordon's voice. Something had to be done.

"I'd be glad to do the demos for you," I said, "but I have classes to teach. I could do them in the summer, though."

"Just write a book, why don't you?"

"Hah! As if I didn't have enough to do!"

"Well, I've told the story of how it all began with Daisy so many times that I've not only lost my voice, I think I'm losing my mind as well. I don't know how actors say the same lines night after night without going mad."

"Teachers do it."

"My point exactly," said Gordon, with a wink.

"Get out of here!" I cried, swatting him with my student enrolment binder. "I'm not going to write a book about our cow. You must be crazy!"

I finished the manuscript of *It All Began with Daisy* about four months later. I sent it out to a handful of publishing companies both here and in New York, feeling confident that the offers would soon come rolling in. I even indulged in a few daydreams about how I would choose the publisher most likely to be the best partner in this endeavor.

Sure enough, a few weeks later some return envelopes showed up in our mailbox down by the road. I opened the first one with trembling hands, eager to read the editor's thoughtful and enthusiastic response to my literary effort. To my profound astonishment the reply turned out to be a form letter telling me that my book did not suit their "list."

My first rejection slip! I soon discovered that the other publishing houses must have been in collusion, for their letters said essentially the same thing. Why were they all so willing to turn me down without spending the time to read the manuscript (the pages were completely smooth at the edges), and what was this mysterious list they referred to with such remarkable unanimity? I shrugged and sent the manuscript out to another dozen publishers.

As the months wore on I ended up with enough rejection slips to paper my bathroom, which, as one of my colleagues at Dalhousie told me, was *sine qua non* for any writer worth her salt. I went home and doggedly assembled yet another dozen manuscripts which I dragged to the post office.

"You'll spend more on postage than you'll ever get back in book sales," said the Lunenburg postmistress, eyeing me with curiosity. "I'd have given up long ago."

Sending out the manuscripts and reading the inevitable rejection slips had eventually become a part of my weekly routine. Sometimes I suspected that there had to be a better way of getting a book published, but I had no idea what that could be. I felt I had no choice but to depend on the law of averages. Surely the manuscript would *have* to fall into the right hands sooner or later!

Snaring the unwary editor

In early September those hands came knocking on my kitchen door. They were owned by an attractive woman with straight, shoulder-length blond hair and a trim Jane Fonda figure. She was trying to track down some home-made ice cream that she had heard about from someone in town.

"You've come to the right place!" I said, inviting her in.

She stepped into the kitchen, glancing with amusement at the old Sweda ice cream machine standing in the corner next to the chest freezer.

"Why aren't you making the ice cream over there?" she said, pointing through the window at the yogurt factory.

"The health inspectors won't let me make an uncultured product in the same place where we manufacture yogurt," I replied. "Cross contamination. But that's okay by me, because I'm glad to be in the house with my children."

The woman looked at the ceiling and smiled knowingly as she heard the thumping strains of rock music coming from a distant bedroom.

"You have a dandy little operation here," she said. "I hope you stay small. You should keep this place a secret."

"You have no idea how horrible it is to be small," I told her. "It's slave labor. Nobody makes new machinery small enough for us, so we have to do everything by hand."

"But at least you're out here in the country, and you have green meadows and ocean views to look at from your windows. I envy you."

"So what sort of work do you do in New York?"

"I'm an editor with one of the publishing companies."

I stared at her. "You're an *editor?* Where do you work?"

"Doubleday. Why?"

"You're an editor at Doubleday, and you're standing here in my kitchen!"

She looked baffled. "Is there something I should know about this kitchen?"

"It's just that I've written a book and…"

"Oh, no!" she interrupted. "You and every fourth person in the world!"

"What? Are there that many writers running around?"

"A lot of people seem to *think* they're writers, I'm afraid. We get about a thousand manuscripts a week. I wish there were as many readers as there are would-be writers."

"What do you do with so many manuscripts?" I asked, handing her a cone with a scoop of rum and raisin ice-cream made with real Bacardi rum.

"What *can* we do?" she said, plunking her handbag down on our portable dishwasher while she took the cone from my hand. "They come pouring in over the transom and they land right in the slush pile. So we send them back. If they have stamped, self-addressed envelopes, that is."

"Don't you ever read them?"

"What's the point?" she said, licking the ice-cream. "We don't have time to read a thousand manuscripts just to find a good one that's publishable."

"How do you know they're bad if you don't read them?"

"If they were any good they'd come through agents," she said, seeing where my questions were leading and looking less friendly by the minute.

"How does a writer get an agent, then?" I persisted.

"You can't just send them your work," she said, taking a more substantial bite of the ice cream and pausing to savor it for a moment. "Agents don't have time to go through all those manuscripts, either."

"Then what does a new writer do?"

"You'd have to move to New York," she said, eyeing me dubiously. "You'd have to get a job with a publishing company and befriend an editor there, or else you'd have to do the cocktail circuit and get to know people."

"I can't move to New York. I have cows to milk, and kids to take care of, and yogurt to worry about. Isn't there some other way I could get an agent?"

"Someone would have to recommend you," she said, biting into the cone and finishing off the ice-cream.

I gazed at her with wide, yearning, calf-like eyes.

"Don't even ask," she said. "I don't know your work."

"I have my manuscript right here," I said, pulling it from the desk drawer in the hallway and waving it triumphantly aloft. She looked horrified.

"I'm on *vacation*," she said, backing away as if she were a vampire being threatened with a sprig of garlic. "I don't read manuscripts when I'm on vacation."

I felt mortified. I was alienating the only editor I had ever met who was in a position to help me get *Daisy* published. How could I persuade her that it was really worth reading? It's one thing to show customers at a demo that the proof of the yogurt is in the eating. That takes one minute. But how does a writer manage to get an editor to invest a whole *day* in reading a manuscript? Nothing came to mind.

"You want me to give you the best advice you'll ever get?" said the editor, looking a bit friendlier as she wiped her lips with the napkin I had given her.

"Sure!" I chirped, eager to hear what she had to say. Any scrap of advice would be welcome to a writer like me who had nowhere to turn.

"Stick to what you're good at," she said solemnly. "Now, this rum and raisin ice-cream is the best I've ever tasted. It's superb. You'll succeed very well if you just keep on making it the way you're doing it. Don't change the recipe."

Having uttered those sound words of advice she turned and headed for the back door. I watched helplessly as my destiny prepared to leave my kitchen.

There was nothing for it but to spring into action. I ran in front of her and blocked her way. She looked at me aghast.

"What are you doing?" she said, in a half threatening, half fearful tone.

"I... I can't let you leave," I stammered.

"What do you mean, you can't let me leave?" she said, staring at me in disbelief. "What's the matter with you? You can't hold me here against my will. What are you doing? Are you *sequestering* me?"

"I never thought of it that way," I admitted, hesitating for a moment. "But I guess you're right."

"This is absurd," she said, attempting to push me aside. But my muscles were used to real work, not just workouts, and I managed to prevail.

"Get out of my way!" she said, raising her voice.

"I can't," I replied, as humbly as possible. "Not till you promise to read my manuscript."

"Nothing like this has ever happened to me before!"

"Well, you've never met a desperate author, then."

"Give me that thing," she said, snatching the manuscript from my hands. "Now stand aside!"

I obeyed at once. She stormed out of the kitchen, letting the door slam behind her. A moment later the door opened abruptly and she marched back in again, made straight for the portable dish washer, grabbed her handbag, gave me a withering look, and was gone.

CHAPTER FOUR

Perception Becomes Reality

Daisy gets an assist

Two days later I was putting away the last of the supper dishes when I suddenly heard Vicki's voice calling from upstairs. "Mom, telephone! It's for you! It's that woman you kidnapped. She wants to talk to you. She sounds kind of excited."

I wiped my hands and looked anxiously at the kitchen extension. The Doubleday editor had probably complained to the local Mounties about my outlandish behavior and was calling to tell me, in gloating, self-satisfied tones, that she would see me in court. What would happen to me? Can you go to jail for holding an editor captive in your kitchen? Could I plead with the jury to have mercy on me for what was really, after all, a crime of passion? Could I ever convince them that an author who puts her heart and soul into writing a book can feel passionately discouraged about being rejected dozens and dozens of times? I picked up the phone with a trembling hand.

"Sonia?" said the editor's familiar voice. "I read your book. I just couldn't put it down. It's the needle in the haystack that every editor dreams of! I'm sending it to the senior editor at Doubleday, and I'm sure she'll want to talk to you about an advance. Don't send it to anyone else!"

"Okay," I croaked, choking back my astonishment. "Don't worry. You can have it. It's yours."

"Where did you get the energy to work like that? And those characters! Does Travis Oickle still live next door? Did he ever get that wall switcher? And the customer at the health food store who thought farming was quaint! She should come and work with *you* for a while! And what ever became of the young man from Quebec who had such long legs he could step right over the backs of the cows? ... Sonia? Are you there?"

I was so taken aback I didn't know what to say or which question to answer first. It didn't seem to matter, because she kept right on talking.

"It's hilarious, you know, a professor with a PhD from Harvard making yogurt and mucking out pigs. You should invite your Harvard friends to get off their high horses and come and milk the cows. They'd get a kick out of Travis. Look, I've got another call waiting so I'll get back to you soon, okay? You'll hear from the senior editor in a few days. I can't wait to see your book in print!"

Beaten by the border patrol

It was three months before I heard anything from Doubleday. I finally got a call from the senior editor who told me she had enjoyed the book, but unfortunately they wouldn't be able to publish it.

"Really?" I said, feeling a little stab of disappointment. "Why?"

"Well, your business is in Canada, you see, and nobody down here is really all that interested in what goes on up there. No offense, but our readers want to know about success stories that take place in the *States*. Things aren't the same in Canada. Our readers want information that they can apply to their lives down *here*."

"But small businesses all face the same problems! Canada is no different. Why should it matter where it takes place?"

"Look, you may be right, but I don't have time to argue the point. We've had our meetings and we've made our decisions. Sales and Marketing aren't willing to take it on. But we're going to send your manuscript to our office in Toronto. I'm sure they'll be more than happy to publish your book. It's well written, and it has local appeal. It should do very well up there."

Another three months went by before I heard anything from the Toronto offices. It was February when I finally got the call.

"Mrs. Jones? This is Doubleday Canada calling. We've read your book, and we think it's terrific. But we're not going to be able to publish it, I'm afraid."

"What? Why not?"

"May I tell you the truth?"

"Of course!"

"Well, our readers are interested in reading success stories about Canadians. But you're an *American*, you see, and…"

It was no use. I argued as long as I dared, but their Sales and Marketing department had made their decision and there was absolutely nothing I could do.

"Don't just lie down and die," said Gordon at the supper table that night. "Why don't you phone your editor friend and tell her how it all turned out?"

"The one that Mom kidnapped?" said Vicki, wide-eyed.

"You could lure her up here again," Valerie suggested, "and this time you could hold her for *ransom*."

I glanced at my 14-year-old daughter and smiled. The child would go far.

"Once bitten, twice shy," I said. "I'm sure she's much too smart to darken my kitchen door again."

I took my family's advice and called the editor from Doubleday that afternoon. She was surprised and annoyed to hear that her company had rejected the manuscript on both sides of the border.

"This is totally absurd," she said, pausing for a moment to collect her thoughts. "I'm not going to let this happen. Something has got to be done about that book. We can't just let it lie around in a drawer. Look, if Doubleday doesn't want it, then... can you keep a secret?"

"You'd rather I didn't tell anyone that Doubleday turned me down?"

"No, it's not that. I'm thinking of doing something a bit unusual. It's not unethical, but it's better not to mention it to anyone."

"Okay," I said, wondering where this was going. "I won't say a word to anyone."

"I have a friend who's an agent. We've worked together for years. Now, if my company doesn't want your book, I see no reason why I shouldn't hand over your manuscript to her. She'll have no trouble placing it with another house."

"Okay then, go for it!"

"Once the book is published you'll be asked to tell the story on talk shows and interviews. And that's okay, but just don't mention my name. We have a whole army of editors here at Doubleday and we all come and go and move around and get other jobs, so if you don't tell anybody who I am then nobody will ever guess."

"I won't. I promise."

"It's too bad, really," she said glumly. "I should be getting some Brownie points for this one."

But she was kind enough to make it possible for me to win some very significant points myself, and I was grateful for her generous assist (always the sign of a great player).

Packaging the product

Within a very short time the agent friend of my nameless benefactor placed my book with E.P. Dutton, one of the top ten publishing companies in New York (later purchased by Penguin). Once the book was in print I was sent on a promotional tour to New York, Philadelphia, Chicago, Minneapolis, Denver, San Francisco, Vancouver, and Toronto. I was interviewed by the major TV networks on their morning news broadcasts and by radio stations and newspapers in both the U.S. and Canada, yet the citizenship and cross-border issues that had kept Doubleday from publishing my book were never once mentioned. The tempest had died, unnoticed, in the depths of the teapot.

During the promotional tour I spent a good deal of my time waiting in green rooms, where I observed the comings and goings of an assortment of celebrities. They invariably arrived in slow-moving limos, surrounded by an entourage of people whose job was to pamper their clients and make them seem impressive. The celebrities came dressed in a startling variety of unusual clothes calculated to make them look, I supposed, creatively eccentric.

"You'll never be a writer, Mom," my daughter Valerie said one day, after returning from a writer's conference that she had attended with her English class. "No, wait. I should phrase that differently. You'll never be a *published* writer, because you don't *look* like a writer, that's why. You look like a *mom*. But the women writers at the conference were tall and skinny, and they wore big hats and lots of make-up and huge glasses. They were very imposing, you know what I mean? Unapproachable, sort of. They made you feel as though they were too important to talk to. You should develop a persona, Mom. You need to package yourself, or nobody will ever take you seriously."

The celebrities I met on the book tour certainly knew about the importance of cultivating their images. My daughter was right. I was a woeful failure when it came to packaging myself. It all reminded me of a bewildering job interview I had once been given in California when I applied for a position teaching Spanish at a small college there.

"You don't look like a Spanish teacher," the interviewer had said, peering at me over his glasses.

"What does a Spanish teacher look like?" I asked, with genuine curiosity.

"I don't know," he replied.

"Then how do you know I don't look like one?"

He became defensive, changed the subject, and brought the meeting to a rapid close. It was the shortest, most bizarre job interview I had ever had. I obviously didn't look like a Spanish professor. I looked like a mom. Marketing was already taking over the world, and perception had become reality.

Even though Daisy knew nothing at all about packaging herself, she generally stole the show in spite of everything. The story of her quiet contribution to the growth and development of the yogurt industry in Eastern Canada was irresistible to the talk show hosts. The book tour was a great success for both of us.

The old-fashioned way

The one thing that Gordon and I hadn't counted on was the unusually broad scope of that success. Shortly after the book came out it was condensed by the *Reader's Digest,* translated into over a dozen languages and circulated among 28,000,000 subscribers. We received letters from people in such far-flung places as Singapore and Nairobi, wanting to know where they could find Peninsula Farm yogurt in their part of the world. Daisy had gone global.

"This is what happens when a small company markets its products to too broad an audience," Gordon said one morning as he flipped through the day's correspondence. "It's gratifying, of course, to see Daisy achieve celebrity status, but it's not going to do us much good. We're in no position to distribute our yogurt to people all over the world. We'll have to leave that to the hordes of business school graduates who want to put out some sort of ersatz McYogurt laced with preservatives and artificial everything. God help us."

"I'm writing a letter to a woman in Sri Lanka who wants to know how to start a yogurt company just like ours," I said.

"Tell her to read your book," said Gordon. "It's a perfect case study of a typical small venture start-up. A book like yours could be very useful to people in developing countries who want to make a contribution to their economy. It's not just about selling yogurt. It's about improving the quality of life."

I opened the next stack of envelopes and sorted them into "how do I make it?" and "where do I find it?" Gordon started another pile for people who just plain enjoyed the book and wanted to wish us well. We went to sleep that night with a sense of solidarity with all the small farmers and entrepreneurs around the world who understood what it means to work hard, to make a good, healthy product, and to sell it at a fair price. We were making our living the old-fashioned way, and we felt deeply gratified by the whole process.

The phony phrozen yogurt phenomenon

My daughter Vicki licked the Peach Melba frozen yogurt from her lips and tried to wipe the drippings off her sleeve. We had been working all afternoon to perfect this new flavor, and neither of us had any appetite left for supper. At least we had the satisfaction of knowing we were the only company making real frozen yogurt.

I had discovered this rather astonishing fact several months before when I decided to test the bacterial count of the frozen yogurt put out by one of my competitors. I knew the company didn't make regular fresh yogurt, so I wondered how they were able to produce frozen yogurt. To my amazement I found that the bacteria count in their so-called frozen yogurt was so low that it obviously didn't contain any yogurt at all. I called the Department of Consumer and Corporate Affairs and asked them why the company was allowed to call its product "frozen yogurt" when it clearly contained no yogurt at all.

"There doesn't have to be any yogurt in frozen yogurt," I was told.

"What was that you said? Frozen yogurt doesn't have to contain yogurt?" I was sure I hadn't heard him correctly.

"That's right. There are no government standards for the definition of either yogurt or frozen yogurt. So as long as the dairies add even a pinch of yogurt starter to their mix they are allowed to call it "frozen yogurt."

Yogurt starter consists of active lactic bacteria collected by a microbiology lab and packaged in a small quantity of powdered milk. The starter is then frozen and stored until it is purchased by a yogurt manufacturer who uses it to inoculate a vat of warm, pasteurized milk. The milk is incubated at a certain temperature for a period of time. The bacteria, which have previously been kept in a state of "suspended animation" in the freezer, slowly come to life again when they find themselves in such ideal conditions. Once they are revived by the warm milk they start multiplying with embarrassing enthusiasm, breaking down the lactose and thickening the milk as they frolic in the vat. After a few hours of this joyful, unrestrained behavior, the milk thickens and becomes yogurt.

"I don't understand," I said to the bureaucrat at the Department of Consumer and Corporate Affairs. "If the manufacturers of frozen yogurt don't use that pinch of starter to inoculate milk and incubate it for a while and make it into yogurt, how can they call their product 'frozen yogurt'? It doesn't contain any yogurt at all. It only contains yogurt *starter,* which isn't the same thing."

"I'm just quoting you the regulations. If the frozen dairy confection can be proven to have any yogurt bacteria in it, no matter how few, it can be labeled *frozen yogurt.*"

"Okay then, so I could make a huge wheel of mozzarella cheese and then insert a tiny fleck of Penicillium into it *after* it's in the cooler, and I'd be allowed to call it blue cheese?"

"I think you're only allowed to call it blue cheese if it's actually made in France. There are laws about that. It's kind of like champagne that way…"

"My point is that the mold wouldn't spread through the cheese and color it or cause blue veins to appear, nor would the cheese taste like blue cheese. It would be bland, sort of like mozzarella. So you can't call mozzarella cheese "blue cheese" just because you put one mold spore in one corner of it! If people bought blue cheese that didn't smell or taste or look like blue cheese, they'd know right away they'd been defrauded."

"I know, I know," said the government official wearily. "But there's no way we can regulate frozen yogurt. We don't have the time be counting bacteria. We don't have the budget, either. So as long as there are two or three active lactic bacteria in the ice-milk mix, we have to allow them to call it yogurt, even if the milk hasn't been inoculated and the bacteria haven't multiplied. Anyway, there's no harm being done to the consumer. The Health Department will tell you the same thing."

"But people think they're eating yogurt and getting the benefits of yogurt. Not everyone has a clear idea of what those benefits are. But they know yogurt is good for them, so that's why they buy it. Does that seem right to you?"

"Mrs. Jones, if I had to worry about all the things that don't seem right to me, I'd have ulcers by now. Those are the regulations. I don't make them, I just enforce them."

"But the dairies shouldn't be allowed to call their product 'frozen yogurt.' They should be made to spell it differently, like *Froot Loops*, for example, which has no fruit in it. They should spell it 'phrozen' yogurt, or something like that, so people will know they're not getting the real thing."

"It's not up to me to decide how names and titles should be spelled," said the official. "Now, if you'll excuse me... I don't have time to count bacteria, and I don't have time to talk about spelling the names of dairy products, either."

The lack of regulations governing yogurt puts Peninsula Farm at a distinct disadvantage. Not only does it take us an extra day of costly labor to make a vat of yogurt before turning it into frozen yogurt, but many customers actually prefer the pseudo frozen yogurt because it's cheaper and it doesn't have a tart flavor. Once again the marketing boys have managed to come up with a clever way to deceive the consumer.

It's all in the perception.

What is going on in the world of yogurt manufacturing? What, in fact, are the large producers calling "yogurt"? If the Department of Consumer and Corporate Affairs doesn't have time to police the bacteria count in products that call themselves frozen yogurt, why can't they at least demand that frozen yogurt be made from real yogurt in the first place?

I'm appalled that manufacturers are allowed to put what they call "frozen yogurt" on the market when in fact the product contains only a small pinch of uncultured yogurt starter, which they have the temerity to call "active lactic cultures." They aren't lying, strictly speaking, for where two or three live bacteria are gathered together, there too, is a miniscule quantity of active lactic culture. So legalism protects misleading perceptions and disguises them as out-and-out lies.

This situation reminds me of a time when I discovered, to my infinite annoyance, that our competitors were using a fruit concoction in their product containing dyes, artificial flavors, and chemical preservatives, but none of these additives were mentioned in their list of ingredients. I discovered this quite by accident when a fruit salesman came to our door toting a plastic bucket filled with a bright red strawberry mixture whose label mentioned these very additives.

I took one look at the list of ingredients and would have politely sent him on his way had he not boasted that a number of well-known yogurt companies bought this mixture from him (he evidently assumed that I would be impressed). I knew for a fact that the list of ingredients on their yogurt containers mentioned only "strawberries," and not the dye, the artificial flavor, or the preservatives used by the salesman's firm in the fruit preparation they sold to the yogurt companies. It looked to me as though we had another situation where the fruit on the label should be spelled incorrectly to warn the consumer it was phony.

"Froot-flavored phrozen yogurt" seemed appropriate to me.

I called the Department of Consumer and Corporate Affairs and asked why the yogurt manufacturers weren't required to list the ingredients in the fruit preparation.

"It would be impossible for us to demand such a thing," I was told. "If all the food manufacturers were required to list the ingredients in their ingredients, the list would stretch from here to China."

"But we cook our own fruit and we don't use any chemical additives at all, so when we say 'strawberries' on our label we mean just that. Strawberries."

"Well, I don't see anything wrong with that," said the man from Consumer and Corporate Affairs.

"Of course, but when our competitors say *strawberries* they're not mentioning the dye, the artificial flavor, and the preservatives. And the mixture is cooked for them in advance, which saves them a whole day of labor. No wonder their prices are lower than ours. And no wonder they have so much more money than we do to make attractive deals with the chains."

"I don't know about that," the man said. "But I do know they're beginning to go to all natural flavors now. So at least that's a step in the right direction."

"They call it all natural flavors, but they neglect to mention they extract that flavor from stems, and skins, and bruised spots, and any other part of the fruit that can't otherwise be sold. Then they cook it all up and extract the flavor by an alcohol process so when they're through with it they have a so-called natural extract that tastes sort of like a mixture of martinis and eau-de-cologne."

"Well, that's their business, not mine. They can do what they like as long as the consumer isn't being harmed in some way."

We had come full circle. Once more the official thinking seemed to maintain that if the consumer isn't being harmed by ice milk parading as frozen yogurt, by strawberries containing red dye, or by natural flavors extracted from substandard fruit, then all was well with the world. It was of no particular concern to the folks over at Consumer and Corporate Affairs that the consumer was being deceived by marketing ploys that concealed the truth. Heaven forbid that our food labels should stretch from here to China! Or that our food even *come* from China, for that matter.

Little did I know at the time that the CCA's flexible attitude to food labeling would be far less of a problem for Peninsula Farm than the overly zealous legalism that was to be displayed by another branch of the federal government in the not-too-distant future.

CHAPTER FIVE

Daisy Goes to Hollywood

Daisy's brush with the bigwigs

I was in the kitchen making yogurt one morning when the phone rang. Since I couldn't pick up right away, Vicki took the call in her bedroom. Soon I heard her thumping down the stairs, calling my name. Her voice sounded urgent.

"Mom, a Hollywood producer wants to talk to you," she said breathlessly. "Pick up!"

I wiped my hands on my apron and went to the living room. Vicki's eyes were full of curiosity and excitement as she handed me the phone. A mellifluous voice greeted me over a static line.

"*Hello,* Mrs. Jones. Yes indeed, I'm really a Hollywood producer. I just had a delightful chat with your daughter. Wonderful child. Look, I've read your book and my people want to make a movie out of it. What do you think about *that*?"

"Well…"

"We've got it all figured out. We've even picked the actors."

The producer named two well-known TV stars and asked me if I was okay with the idea of having them play the roles of Gordon and me.

"Sure, they'd be fine of course," I said, a bit hesitantly. They were both excellent actors, but it was somehow hard for me to imagine them on a farm in Nova Scotia, working the land shoulder-to-shoulder with each other in sickness and in health, in good weather and bad, and never giving up no matter what the circumstances. What would they do without the usual amenities of urban living? I couldn't picture them lasting very long with the well running dry and the power going out, while forty quarts of milk lurked somewhere in the kitchen waiting to be processed.

"Believe it or not we've already got them both lined up. They're very excited about the project. They just adore underdogs, and they're great with horses, too."

"No horses. Just cows."

"Whatever. They'll work with cows. So what do you say?"

"Well, there are quite a lot of things to discuss."

"Don't sweat the small stuff. I'll send you a contract."

"That'll be a good start. I'll have to see it on paper, though, before I can give you an answer. Hello?"

The phone was dead. The Hollywood producer had hung up.

There was a lot of excitement around the dinner table that night. The girls couldn't wait to hear all about the movie.

"When are they going to start shooting?" Valerie asked.

"I don't know," I said. "I haven't signed the contract."

"Are famous movie actors really going to come up here to visit our farm?" Vicki asked.

"Maybe. But don't get your hopes up. I haven't agreed to anything yet."

It wasn't long before a weighty and rather daunting movie contract arrived in the mail. It was a long document containing many terms and conditions that made me feel rather nervous. I wished my father could have been there to advise me, but he had died many years before from a heart attack brought on by the hostile takeover of Technicolor Films Limited, where he had served as Managing Director of European operations for over thirty years.

It all happened very suddenly. He was awakened early one morning by a phone call from a lawyer informing him that the company now belonged to a consortium which held the majority of Technicolor's stocks. My father was shocked. He tried his best to organize a proxy fight, but to no avail. After soldiering on for a couple of years, his health began to fail. He felt personally responsible for not foreseeing the takeover and for not being able to do anything about it. He suffered three stress-related heart attacks and was finally felled by the fourth one in 1963. It was an unbearably sad ending to a career dedicated whole-heartedly to the welfare of an extraordinary, ground-breaking company.

I peered at the Hollywood contract that I held in my hands, hating the legal style and the hard-nosed tone. The lawyers who had drawn up the document seemed to feel it was necessary to take every imaginable precaution to protect the parties on their end from all the conniving schemes I was likely to dream up. It was apparently my job to write in the clauses for my own protection.

"So you want to buy all the rights to my book," I said to the producer the next morning, seeking clarification. "Does that mean you want the right to use the names of real people? Like David Sobey, for instance?"

"You bet."

"And does it mean you'll have the right to say anything you like about him, and change things around however you see fit?"

"Look, when we buy the rights it means just that. The rights belong to us. We don't like authors getting in the way after the deal's been made. No offense, but authors can be a royal you-know-what. They object to everything and waste our time, and time is extremely expensive in Hollywood."

"What do they object to?"

"They say things like 'I never said that,' or 'this never happened at all.' They don't want us to change anything.

But *we're* the professionals.   We know what we're doing.
We know what sells and what the audience wants to see."
    "So are you going to change *It All Began with Daisy?*"
    "For sure.   It's too bland.   There's no sex, for one
thing."
    "No sex?   That's not exactly true!   What about the time
we put the neighbor's bull in with our cows?"
    The producer was not amused.
    "People want to see conflict."
    "Gordon and I had to face plenty of conflict."
    "Sure, but the two of you weren't at each other's throats.
Who's going to believe that?   Besides, the audience wants
knock down, drag out fights."
    "Stress doesn't always drive people apart.   Sometimes it
draws them together.   Anyway, that's the way it happened."
    "See?   Just what I said.   Authors always want the movie
to be exactly the way it happened in real life.   But real life is
usually extremely dull, and that's not what sells at the box
office.   We need something that'll knock 'em dead."
    "So what did you have in mind?"
    "Come clean with me, now.   You can't tell me all that
stress didn't push one or the other of you into an affair or
something.   I wasn't born yesterday."
    "No, it definitely did not drive either of us into an
affair."
    "There you go.   You want us to make the movie exactly
the way it happened to you.   Well, for one thing Puritanism
went out with the dinosaurs.   And for another thing, real life
doesn't go over very well in a movie theater.   It has to be
bigger than life.   Things have to go wrong.   Then they have
to get worse.   Then they have to look hopeless.   You and
Gordon separate, get a divorce, what have you.   The kids go
nuts.   They get hooked on drugs."
    "Right, and when the movie comes out we'll be walking
down the street and our friends will see us and say, *oh hello,
I thought you two were divorced!   How nice to see you
together again.*   Thanks a lot."

"You want a movie made about you? You have to pay the price."

"Why does it have to be about *me*? Why don't you get your screenwriters to make up some sort of a story about a sexy *fictional* character?"

"People want true stories."

"But it won't *be* a true story when your screenwriters get through with it!"

"What's the difference? Who'll know? We'll say it's *based* on a true story. People will come to visit your farm. They'll want to see a cow. A real live cow."

It's all in the perception. Reality is now virtual reality.

"Listen, don't be so nit-picky," he went on. "We come up there and make a movie, you'll get lots of publicity. It's good for tourism and good for business."

"Good for *my* business?"

"Whose business do you think I'm talking about?"

"How do I know that you won't end up destroying my business? David Sobey has been very good to me. He's my benefactor, actually. So if you say anything bad about him, it wouldn't be fair. Can I get a clause in the contract to protect the reputations of real people in the book?"

"I can't promise you anything. It all depends on how the screenwriters decide to deal with it. I don't want to tie their hands."

"Well, can I talk to the screenwriters, then?"

"What's the point? When you sign over the rights, they belong to us."

"Then I don't think I'll be able to go through with it."

"Are you nuts? You'd turn down fifty thousand bucks?"

"I'd lose more than that if I lost the good will of the people in Nova Scotia who helped me. And there were quite a few, believe me."

"You're not getting out of it that easy, Sis" he growled, in a menacing voice. "You made a legally binding verbal contract with me over the phone."

"A legally binding verbal contract? About what? The only thing we talked about on the phone was the main casting. But there are lots of terms and conditions in the contract itself that I can't agree to. Anyway, wasn't it Sam Goldwyn who said that a verbal contract isn't worth the paper it's written on?"

"You want to test me?" he said. "Go ahead. I'll take you to court and sue you for all you're worth. By the time I'm through with you there won't even *be* a Peninsula Farm to make a movie about."

He hung up, leaving me standing there with my heart pounding. I called my lawyer immediately and told him what had happened.

"You have to be prudent in cases like these," he said, after listening carefully to all the details of my story. "I don't know for sure, but your intellectual property could be encumbered. I'm not an expert in this field, though. I think you should contact a specialist in entertainment contract law. I'd try some place like Toronto."

The bark of legal beagles

The entertainment contract lawyer in Toronto agreed that the situation required some very serious consideration. He would have to go to Osgood Hall, he said, to see if he could dig up some precedents. He'd have to contact the producer who talked to me on the phone, too.

"I might even have to make a couple of trips to the West Coast, to Hollywood. It'll all take time."

"Well, how much will all that cost?"

"It's hard to say. But I assure you, it's worth it to you to pay for legal protection in a matter like this."

"And I suppose I'll have to pay all your expenses."

"Of course! But as I said before, you're doing the right thing. I have the experience, and you need the protection."

"Just don't stay in the Beverly Hills Hotel, if you don't mind."

"Everything's expensive in L.A. But I'm an honest man. I'll do my best to keep the costs down, but I'm not exactly a HoJo type guy, you know what I mean?"

"This is all just plain ridiculous!" I blurted out. "I didn't agree to anything during my phone conversation with that Hollywood producer except that I'd be perfectly happy to work with the actors he talked to me about. We spoke for three minutes. He can't claim that I verbally agreed to all the terms and conditions in the contract during that short period of time. If he tries to say that I made a legally binding verbal agreement, then tell him to send you the twelve-hour phone bill to prove it! Call his bluff!"

"It's not that simple," said the Toronto lawyer soberly.

"Why not? It ought to be as simple as pie!"

"I don't want to take anything for granted at this point. The proper thing for me to do is to look into the case from every angle to ensure that you're not liable for anything in the eyes of the law."

"No judge would take that producer's claim seriously. He'd throw the case out. It doesn't make sense."

"There are a lot of cases that don't look as if they could ever hold up in court, yet many people are sued by perfect idiots and they end up losing their shirts. Do you want to take that chance?"

"But it's not logical."

"Who ever said the law was logical?"

"Well, I need to know how much it's going to cost for you to look into all this."

"As I said, I can't tell you that in advance. It depends on what I find out during the course of my investigation. But it would be unprofessional of me to leave any stone unturned. I like to give my clients the best advice money can buy."

The entertainment contract lawyer immediately delved into the complicated and legally-binding entanglements that he believed were likely to emerge from my short, truncated telephone conversation with the rather unsavory Hollywood producer.

He turned out to be so professional, in fact, that it wasn't until four months and $23,500 later that he finally came to the unquestionably brilliant conclusion that my book was indeed unencumbered, just as I had told him right from the start. I decided to consult my lawyer in Halifax again about whether I should contest his exorbitant charges. His bill, at that time, represented more than a year's salary for me at Dalhousie.

"That sum of money is indeed very considerable for the amount of work he did for you," my lawyer agreed. "I believe that in all likelihood he treated himself to a bit of an education at your expense, and maybe a little entertainment on the side, too."

"Nice. You know, I never could pin him down about what the final, overall cost would be. Not even a ball park figure. And then when he sent me the bill, I couldn't get him to itemize anything. What do you think I should I do?"

"I don't think it would be wise for you to challenge him. By the time you pay all the costs involved, you'll conclude that you'd have been better off just paying the bill and getting on with your life. It's not worth it taking a lawyer to court. It's nothing but grief and misery."

Daisy's brush with Hollywood was over and I was a little wiser, but I would have been a lot happier if the cost of this totally gratuitous experience hadn't been quite so high.

CHAPTER SIX

Moving Forward

On the road again

The funny farm hit the road again with the same sense of expectation that it had exhibited in years past when our company first attracted attention by becoming a modestly successful small business enterprise. I use the term "modestly" because we were just barely successful enough to survive in a highly competitive business environment, but never quite successful enough to have to pay taxes.

However that may be, it has long been the policy of the various local political parties to encourage entrepreneurship in the Maritime provinces, for it's well known that the majority of jobs that exist in this region are created by the small business community. It's also an unfortunate fact that a high percentage of these small enterprises go out of business with monotonous regularity.

But Daisy was becoming well known in the province, and would-be entrepreneurs wanted to know how they could learn from her example. Since our little company was still managing to survive in spite of everything, I was invited to lecture on small business management and new venture startups at a number of high schools and universities, as well as numerous service clubs, government-sponsored seminars, commodity producer associations, and various private sector conventions.

To my great relief I discovered that public speaking was not the scary experience I expected it to be. On the contrary,

I thoroughly enjoyed the opportunity of meeting people who shared my interests and contributed informative comments in the question-and-answer periods after the presentations.

I didn't always have an easy time understanding the people who took the microphone during those question-and-answer periods, however. One evening, after addressing a large group of farmers who were visiting from Australia, I was presented with a question that left me feeling completely baffled.

"Do you have chaos on your farm?" asked one of the visitors. He had slipped into the conference room at the last minute and had been standing at the back, listening with interest to the various questions that were being asked.

I was convinced that he had taken one look at me and quickly deduced that any farm with which I was even loosely associated would inevitably suffer from a significant amount of turmoil and confusion.

"Well, yes," I admitted, smiling bravely. "But my husband is very good at handling all the problems."

"Is that so?" replied the Australian farmer, giving me a quizzical look. "And how many chaos does he milk?"

Even though I remain unconvinced that the world stands to benefit in the long run from globalization, I must admit that I thoroughly enjoy the perspectives offered by people from other nations and cultures.

Once when I was addressing the Commerce Society at Dalhousie, I spotted an Asian student sitting quietly in the third row. I had just received the Chinese version of *It All Began with Daisy,* and I was dying to know how they had translated the title. I asked him if he knew how to render the ideograms in English. When he told me that he thought he could manage the task, I had some students pass my copy of the Chinese version back to him. He studied the title for a little while with sober concentration.

"It says, *The Romance of Little Chrysanthemum.*"

"Really!" I exclaimed, delighted to know how the editors in Taiwan had rendered the title in English. "But why did they change my cow's name from *Daisy* to *Little Chrysanthemum?"*

Necks were craned in his direction. He hunkered down lower in his seat and studied the title once again.

"*Daisy* too common a name for such honorable cow," he said finally.

The students burst into applause.

The only time I was actually terrified at the prospect of addressing the public was when I was invited to speak in French about "La Vache Marguerite" on a TV broadcast in Moncton, New Brunswick. The interviewer spoke French with me on the phone prior to the engagement, assuring me that everything would be just fine.

She turned out to be right, and for two reasons. For one thing, the French accent in New Brunswick is perfectly standard (the Quebecois *Joual* always throws me for a loop). Secondly, I was able to read the French version of *It All Began with Daisy* before the interview so I could refresh my memory about farm vocabulary. What delighted me most of all, however, was that our sales went up in New Brunswick after the interview, making it clear to me once again how important it is to meet people where they live and to speak to them in their own languages. I found myself wondering how often the chief executive officers of Danone and Parmalat came to the Maritime Provinces with that particular purpose in mind.

Perhaps one of my most enjoyable experiences on the road came as a result of my having been invited to represent Maritime business interests at the "Shamrock Summit" in Quebec City. The purpose of the meeting was to meet with President Ronald Reagan to discuss the pros and cons of free trade between Canada and the U.S., a subject that was holding everyone in thrall at that time. Needless to say the free trade agreement was strongly opposed by Canadian dairy interests, since our milk would have been hammered hard by the cheaper milk from south of the border.

Other Canadian businesses, such as those involved in the export of raw materials, were interested in the short-term profits that could come their way through greater access to American markets. Most of the people at my table, however, preferred to adopt a "wait and see" attitude to the free trade proposal, fearing, perhaps, the long-term results of accepting an invitation to go into the American spider's parlor without first checking for cobwebs. I kept my mouth shut and allowed them to think I was a highly circumspect Canadian fly, just like the rest of them. I didn't want to invite any border problems such as the ones I had already encountered with Doubleday.

Gordon's folly

When I got home and discussed the meeting with Gordon, he guffawed at the whole concept of free trade with the U.S.

"Canadians don't stand a chance against the U.S.," he hooted. "All we can do is weaken the loony to make our exports more attractive, but what does that accomplish? We become poorer here at home. And what can we export to them, anyway? Raw materials! There's not enough profit in that. And what are we going to do when we run out of natural resources? We should sell the whole country to the Americans while it's still worth something."

"Gordon!" I exclaimed, drawing in my breath. "Button your lips! Don't let anyone hear you talk like that! If you ever said that out loud you'd be the most unpopular man in Canada!"

"Well, it's not as though I don't care about Canada. But we're selling our country down the river anyway, by giving away our precious natural resources. What do you think is going to happen in the future? We'll get poorer and poorer while the Americans get richer and richer. If they want our raw materials, let them buy the country! Another Seward's folly wouldn't hurt them. Then Ottawa could dole out the purchase price to the citizens, and we'd be laughing!"

"Nobody here will ever, *ever* buy that idea. They'd call it 'Gordon's folly.'"

"I know. Believe me, I know. People always want to protect their culture, and their sovereignty, and all that good stuff. But what does it boil down to? As far as Americans and Canadians are concerned, we have a lot in common. If you look at our history, most of us were just on different sides of a political issue, that's all. Rebels and Loyalists. But so what? Do we want to deal with ever-increasing poverty just because of a dead issue like that?"

"Gordon, you're a complete nut case. People want to live in their own countries. They want to preserve their cultural identity. Separatists are springing up everywhere. Countries are heading in the direction of devolution, not amalgamation!"

"But cultural identity shouldn't be the prime motivating factor. There's already a big cultural difference between people in Maine and people in Alabama. And between New Yorkers and Los Angelinos, too. There's not really that much difference between the two sets of circumstances. Amalgamate the whole shooting match, that's what I say."

"It sounds to me as if you're advocating an Anschluss."

"Yes, and what did Hitler pay for Austria? Zilch. I'm not proposing that the Americans should steal the farmer's goat. I'm saying they should give the poor devil a fair price for the goat. I'm saying that Canada should *sell* the country to the Americans, before it's too late. There'd be enough to ensure the financial comfort of every single family in the nation. It wouldn't be in the least bit unreasonable for everyone to expect to be paid a million dollars for the sale."

"If you say it in public, you'll be tarred and feathered."

"Don't worry. If things keep going the way they're going, nobody but the Chinese and the Indians and the Arabs will be able to afford to buy either the tar or the feathers. When we get done merging Canada and the U.S., we can start with Mexico." Gordon snapped his fingers. "In an instant we would have no more trade problems, no more illegal immigration, we'd all be rich, and Mexico would be Canada's Winter Ocean Playground. What would be wrong with that?"

"So then you're saying that as a big thinker you'd like to include everyone in your merger and acquisition scheme?"

"You bet I would, as long as they adopt the Constitution and the Bill of Rights. I'm getting old and I can't afford to wait for the Christians and Islam to revisit the Crusades, or for the folks in South America to try out communism, or for the loyalists to retreat from the rebels again."

Love thine enemy (but carry a big stick)

I soon had to abandon all my concerns about the strength of the Canadian armed services and the safety of the nation. Another war had broken out on a microscopic level in the yogurt factory. Something was managing to massacre our yogurt bacteria, and I strongly suspected that even the Pentagon itself would be at a loss as to how to deal with it.

"Mom, take a look at this yogurt," Valerie had said, handing me a container. "Dad sent me over to show you a sample. What do you think?"

I inspected the product in the small cup she had brought with her from the factory. The yogurt was thin and translucent, with little white bits floating in it. I had never seen it turn out like that. I began to feel nervous. Was I going to be able to solve this one? My job as a yogurt manufacturer involved protecting some of God's tiniest creatures from their enemies. Any carelessness on my part could expose the yogurt bacteria to competition from hostile microbes that circulate in the air. Or if I let down my guard even for a moment, unwelcome yeasts could settle gleefully on the surface of the finished product, replicating their spores with wanton abandon.

When I began experimenting with yogurt many years ago, I knew nothing about the precarious existence of my diminutive protégés. I learned by trial and error. At first I was so unsuccessful in my attempt to produce marketable yogurt that Gordon had to buy some pigs to eat my mistakes. They were uncritical admirers of all my abortive efforts, devouring the spoiled yogurt with flattering enthusiasm. But eventually I learned the ropes well enough to take the next logical steps toward victory, and everything went smoothly from then on.

But on that fateful day when Valerie showed me the yogurt sample at the breakfast table, I had to face for the first time what every yogurt maker dreads: a total batch failure. When I arrived at the factory I found that all three of our 400-gallon vats contained clumps of white curds floating aimlessly in an ocean of yellow whey. What could have gone wrong? I checked everything. Our tests showed that there were no antibiotics in the milk that we were purchasing from the local dairy. There was no chemical residue in the vats, and the thermometers were correctly calibrated – but still the nightmare continued!

We finally decided to hire a dairy consultant to analyze the problem. He was the most taciturn man on the face of the earth. He refused to make any observations or answer any questions until his investigation was complete. Once he was satisfied with his examination of the process and the product, he turned to me and opened mouth for the first time.

"You have phage," he said tersely.

I stared at him. Phage? I had never heard the word.

"Bacteriophage," he said, assuming the longer word would clarify everything. "Viruses that kill yogurt bacteria."

"Well, how do we get rid of them?"

"You can't. You can steam clean the plant if you like, but some will always survive. They're here to stay. You're lucky you were able to get by as long as you did before they found you. You're pretty isolated out here in the country, though, so you had a good run of phage-free years."

"What do other dairies do about phage?" I asked him.

"You'll have to change your bacterial strains every ten days or so. That way the viruses will have to mutate for about a week to get ready to attack, then you change to another strain and make them mutate again. When they're almost ready for the next assault, you change back to the first strain and so on. Just keep them confused. Make them mutate back and forth between strains as if you were playing a microscopic game of ping-pong."

We've been playing ping-pong ever since, and with gratifying success. But we have found it tedious, expensive, and irritating to have to protect our yogurt bacteria by keeping those miserable little viruses amused. I'd love to be able to kill them off once and for all, but up to this point nobody has found a way to do so. There will certainly be a Nobel Prize some day for the scientists who find a way to cure viral disease.

But wait! Maybe I shouldn't be trying so hard to kill off the viruses of the world. I once read an article about some microbiologists in a remote laboratory in Tbilisi who were using the phage virus to fight pathogenic bacteria that had become resistant to antibiotics. I remember being impressed by this creative new approach to curing diseases caused by deadly bacteria that have "learned" to protect themselves against antibiotics. I felt ashamed of myself for secretly harboring such uncharitable thoughts about phage.

Enemies and predators are all around us, if we look closely enough. They lurk in clever hiding places, they watch with narrowed, calculating eyes, they pounce when we least expect it, they ambush innocent passersby. Just watch the nature programs. The world is full of them. But perhaps we shouldn't be too hasty in bringing out the big guns. Maybe it behooves us to become better acquainted with the ones we consider to be pests or personal adversaries. Who knows, with a little love and nurturing and the occasional game of ping-pong, some of them might turn out to be our new best friends.

CHAPTER SEVEN

Frog in Boiling Water

Kraft Foods or food crafts?

Peninsula Farm Limited enjoyed a real heyday after the publication of *It All Began with Daisy*. As we entered the 1990s the company boasted 25% of the market share in the yogurt category, in spite of the big names of our major competitors. We had a loyal customer base, and sales were beginning to bring in a small profit for the very first time in our history. But if we listened carefully, we could hear the heavy tread of the food giants prowling in the night, seeking whom to destroy.

Maybe I'm misreading it. They weren't really predators. They were like mindless, unstoppable machines pushing ever forward, either absorbing or crushing whatever was in their path, but the repercussions were beginning to be felt even as far away as in tranquil Nova Scotia. As Grand Metropolitan looked hungrily at Pillsbury, and Kraft was gobbled up by Philip Morris, suppliers here were starting to wonder how the new oligopolies emerging in the food industry were going to affect the smaller players in the marketplace.

Nobody was underestimating the control the giants would have over retail shelf space. The Goliaths would demand and get more and more of the prime footage that was already in painfully short supply, while the little Davids of the food world would be pushed over to the less desirable positions or dropped altogether. It wasn't hard to predict that the shelf space squeeze would affect new enterprises and small companies the most, and the battle would get tougher with the consolidation of the big manufacturers.

The signs of the times were getting harder to ignore, especially the case of a fisherman who decided to market his grandmother's recipe for pickled herring. He was one of the few to get into a chain store, but his luck ran out. When he was unable come up with enough money to buy shelf space for his products, the grocery chain's head office marked up his herring to the point where nobody could afford to buy it.

Life can be hard indeed for small independent firms. I remember that I had my share of problems getting my own dairy products onto the shelves years ago. After long months of experimentation, I finally came up with a yogurt that even yogurt haters loved. I was sure that once it was in the stores I would be able to stand back and watch hundreds of happy customers faint in ecstasy at the first taste of my product.

But to my dismay I discovered that the only individuals in the world who are completely impervious to ecstasy of any kind (especially the gourmet kind) are the head buyers of supermarket chains. They tend to be far more interested in their bottom lines than in their taste buds, and they cannot be trusted to salivate except when discussing manufacturers' high rebates or deep discounts.

Those of us who were too small to offer the buyers such tasty morsels found ourselves all too often cooling our heels in outer chambers, our sample cases bursting with mouth-watering delicacies, while salesmen from well-endowed and prestigious corporations were welcomed with open arms into the inner sanctum where all the final deals were struck. What to do? Should the small "boutique" food manufacturers try to imitate their powerful brethren and provide the public with rubber cheese, artificial syrups and phosphorescent cupcakes in order to cut the cost of real ingredients?

I was once given just such advice by a beetle-browed head-office buyer who told me that I could never get into his chain unless I coughed up a suitable "inside program." When I protested that his program wouldn't work for me, he suggested I do what all my competitors did – cut costs by lowering the quality of the product. With the money saved, he said, I could buy several feet of shelf space in the stores. If I didn't like that idea, I could raise the price of my yogurt and use the customers' money to buy my way into the chain. I could see right away that none of it made any sense. If I lowered the quality of my yogurt, I could never hope to compete against the companies that lured their customers with two-for-one sales and cents-off coupons. And as for raising the price of my product, I had already learned that lesson from my friend the herring pickler. I left the buyer's office that afternoon feeling dejected and resentful that the excellence of my product counted for so little in the eyes of the decision-makers.

I did what thousands of small entrepreneurs have done to force an entry into a market geared to megabucks – I started at the bottom. The delicatessens and the health food stores were delighted to get an outstanding product that was genuinely distinguishable from the commercial varieties, and little by little the consumer demand began to build.

Maybe I should have stopped right there. Getting into the chains is not necessarily the panacea for every possible woe, and being vulnerable has always had its drawbacks. Small companies are likely to find that their competitors are eternally poised on the edge of their shelf space, ready to pounce on their territory the moment their backs are turned or their guard is down. They may also discover that there are rotation problems, cooler breakdowns, delivery tie-ups, and arrogant dairy case boys to contend with. It is a given that receivers are always on break, tractor-trailers belonging to competitors take forever to unload, and their products always end up on the eye-level shelf.

Perhaps if I had known all this in advance I never would have tried to get into the chains, but there's a limit to the amount of slave-labor a person can endure. If you don't make enough product to justify a small factory, you are likely to find yourself spending your days dipping yogurt into containers with a soup ladle, affixing the labels onto said containers by hand, and getting maybe four hours' sleep on a good night. A medical resident has it better than that.

But we persisted anyway, holding on by the fingernails, hoping that we would be the ones to survive the pressure of the days ahead when the market became more and more dominated by the giants. It seemed plain to us that the me-too copy-cat companies would be the ones to suffer the most in the coming pinch. We knew that there simply wouldn't be enough shelf space for anything in between. We understood that the market of the next decade would be carved up between Kraft Food and food crafts. We also believed that satisfied customers would root out the products they loved, so we concluded that excellence had to be the clarion call for those Davids who wished to remain in the fight. In those halcyon days of the early '90s, we had no idea what difficult times lay ahead.

Lo-tech, small science

"You'll never make it in today's marketplace," said my nemesis the chain store food buyer. "You can't compete with the hi-tech packaging that's winning your customers' dollars. You don't have the money to invest in science and technology. Why don't you just step aside and enjoy your retirement years?"

It's a common belief here in Nova Scotia that science and technology are costly, arcane pursuits that benefit only such hi-tech industries as aerospace or telecommunications. Since most of us are out there in the trenches making a living in what we consider to be lo-tech or even no-tech fields, we tend to dismiss science and technology as having nothing to do with our needs or interests.

At least that's how I felt when I started my business. Back in the mid 1970s, while my scientific colleagues were working out formulas on the blackboards of our nation's institutes of higher learning, I was working away in my no-tech kitchen trying to figure out ways of making a better yogurt. My life, in fact, was so filled with cows and milk and mad-cap experiments that it never occurred to me that I was engaged in scientific activity until letters began coming in addressed to the "Director of Product Development." I shook my head and chuckled to think how shocked the writers of those letters would be if they ever found out that the Director of Product Development was only me – a mother-housewife-author-professor-entrepreneur – laboring away at the kitchen stove.

As Peninsula Farm grew, our problems and challenges began to multiply too, and Gordon and I both found we were being addressed with all sorts of new and wonderful titles. After designing the layout and workflow plan for our new plant, the construction workers solemnly referred to me as the "Architect." When the agitators in the vats in our new factory refused to stir the yogurt properly, Gordon was suddenly given the vaunted title of Plant Manager. When times and temperatures needed careful attention and delicate adjustments, I found myself wearing the hat of Production Supervisor. When our new filling machine decided to behave itself with about the same decorum as a child in the terrible two's, Gordon tried to be a sensible, scientifically-minded Mechanical Engineer. Back then Gordon worked full time caring for the farm and milking the cows, so he was given the title of Procurement Officer.

It slowly began to dawn on me that business owners are constantly applying science and technology to their various problems, yet they rarely see themselves as being engaged in scientific or technological pursuits. The very sound of the words is scary. Scientists are perceived by the business world as being highly educated specimens in white lab coats who lace their speech with jargon nobody can understand. Besides, what do scientists know about life in the trenches?

But small business people know a good deal more about science than they think. A local ship's engineer with a fourth-grade education offered us some brilliant advice about pumping seawater up to our plant for cooling purposes, but he had no idea that his off-the-cuff ideas could be described as technology transfer. The farmer next door, a fifth-grade dropout, was unaware that he was performing the same feat when he transferred his knowledge of tractor technology to the arcane functions of our refrigeration units.

I stared at the chain store food buyer who was telling me that my unscientific approach to making yogurt was going to be my downfall. Downfall, schmownfall. What gave him the right to predict that my customers were going to trade in real yogurt for an ersatz product wrapped up in a pretty package? He was seriously underestimating the intelligence of Nova Scotians when he said things like that.

I found myself imagining what fun it would be to prove him wrong. My proud little heart relished the moment when this know-nothing man with his undeserved power over me would wake up one day and realize that Peninsula Farm had been producing a yogurt fit for royalty. I wanted him to feel foolish about never having fully appreciated how fortunate his stores were to be carrying our product.

"What are you looking so pleased about?" the buyer frowned. "I'm telling you, you're going to have to get with the program. It's tubes and multipacks and bright colors that count nowadays. You're lucky I'm warning you."

Searching hi and lo for quality

Do you ever have the time to take a leisurely stroll through your friendly neighborhood supermarket? Or are you the late-for-dinner speedy Gonzalez grabbing blindly for grocery items as you go whizzing down the aisles? If you are like me and millions of other beleaguered roadrunners, then caveat emptor! Chances are you're missing some really excellent buys.

Marketing experts in the retail food industry have recently come to the monumental conclusion that working consumers have two distinguishing features: we're smart and we're busy. The first salient characteristic is well known to be a drawback to the manipulators of public opinion – we have long since grown cynical about slick advertising.

But when it comes to our second characteristic, we're putty in the hands of manipulators both large and small. Most children know perfectly well they can get anything they want from their parents if they catch them while they're on the run. And the marketing experts, who are in all probability the grown-up offspring of busy parents, are now applying the same lessons on a professional level. They've made the breathtaking discovery that when consumers move along grocery aisles in excess of thirty miles an hour they rarely have time to raise or lower their gaze by more than an average of nine inches.

Like "prime time" on TV, the eye-level shelf has become a magnet attracting products manufactured by large corporations whose bottom lines are always enhanced by enviable economies of scale. We hardly need be reminded that many of these mega-corporations are located outside the province and often south of the border. But a fair number of Nova Scotian companies, less leonine in power and stature, have learned to compete by adopting the tactics of the mouse that roared. They have fought a brave battle in the arena of excellence, where their small size has given them certain advantages over their ponderous, slow-moving, less creative adversaries.

Some of our dauntless local mice have gnawed their way into public awareness, and their popular products have created enough demand to earn space on the coveted eye-level shelves. But others have not been so fortunate. Many of my favorite food items, ranging from condiments to cookies, have been lovingly produced by local artisans whose work is inspired less by their pocketbooks and more by their highly educated palates. Yet all too often these delectable products have not enjoyed the privilege of being represented on the magic middle shelves.

What to do? We can't all hope to win a place on the middle shelf. But I think I've come up with the perfect solution. I've invented a body-length skateboard on which consumers can lie prone as they propel themselves along supermarket aisles grabbing high-quality but lesser-known local products off the bottom shelves. The skateboard is also equipped with rungs on which the determined shopper can climb to the top shelf for access to the other excellent products hidden thereon.

But before you go rushing out to the store in search of my invention, be advised that this board is not easy to find in retail outlets. It's been carefully stashed out of reach and out of sight by experts whose calculations have declared it to be an item of only marginal profit potential.

Don Quixote rides again

It is a poignant and bitter truth that we human beings are constructed in such a way that we tend to appreciate what we have only after we have lost it or it has been wrested from our grasp. I can't say I was desperately sorry to have opted to retire early from my position as full professor at Dalhousie University. I was, however, a little uncomfortable to have lost my financial safety net, for I was too young at the time to get a pension. The University returned my contributions, of course, but it was up to me to see to it they were wisely invested. Gordon and I suddenly found ourselves entirely responsible for our own economic fate.

I did my best to ponder the lilies of the field and not worry about what the morrow would bring, but there were moments when I equated the image of those lilies with Hamlet's idea that he was lily-livered and lacked gall. What would life be like without a paycheck or a pension? For a while I went around feeling slightly unhinged and a bit nostalgic for the protective wings of Mother Dalhousie.

To my astonishment and great comfort many of my former students were feeling nostalgic, too. I received a number of notes from them telling me how they missed their old friend, Don Quixote. They didn't say anything about missing *me*, mind you, but I was secretly flattered that I had been able to bring Cervantes' fictional character to life with sufficient vividness to provide my students with a sense of loss at the end of my tenure as their professor.

I found myself thinking more and more about the gallant knight from La Mancha, whose uncompromising idealism at first seemed like a form of total insanity to his family and friends. I had taught this great 17th-century Spanish novel for nearly twenty years, and every year I felt deeply moved by the wisdom of his insanity, if indeed insanity it was. He took his knightly calling seriously, and sallied forth with every intention of making his world a better one.

Had God decreed that his destiny was to make yogurt for Manchegans, you can be sure he would have wanted it to be a product of indisputable quality – a gift of pure ambrosia. If the local shopkeeper had refused to let him sell his yogurt to the denizens of his village (whose name nobody could recall, according to Cervantes), he would have ridden his broken-down nag right into that shop and terrified the poor man with his frightening demeanor and uplifted lance. He never would have given up his dream of providing his companions with the best yogurt in all of La Mancha. Had he lived in the 1990s, he would not have been daunted, either, by corporate giants or fire-breathing dairy case boys. He would have castigated anyone who had had the temerity to interfere with him. Nobody could have stopped him in this honorable quest. He would have prevailed. He would have stood tall. And even if the villagers of his day and age hadn't liked his yogurt they would have eaten it with feigned appreciation, while all the time furtively eyeing his noble posture and strong right arm.

Don Quixote, like so many of us, wanted his life to have purpose and to be useful to others, and he dedicated all his waking hours to making sure that it was. All it took was an unbreakable spirit and a willingness to reach for the stars. All that was needed was an indestructible determination to march into hell for a heavenly cause. I could relate. What greater hell than a constant tussle with giant food chains, megalithic multinational conglomerates, or intransigent food inspectors? What more heavenly cause than providing the world with real food made with pure ingredients?

The Knight of the Mournful Countenance, as a local innkeeper once described him, was an inspiration to me as an entrepreneur.

"Why do you do it?" Sancho Panza asks his master in the intelligent musical, *Man of La Mancha*.

Why, indeed? Why did Don Quixote go forth and allow himself to get beaten up by all kinds of unsavory characters every single day of his life?

I was asked the same type of question by a business student during the question-and-answer period after a lecture I had presented at Acadia University.

"Why do you keep on making yogurt when there are so many struggles and so little profit? Why do you do it?"

I thought about his question for a while.

"It's pride," I told him, finally. "Gordon and I get great satisfaction from making a product we can be proud of. It gives us a kind of happiness that money can't buy. It's a form of completely impractical insanity, I guess."

The business student smiled. I knew he'd have loved Don Quixote. As I contemplated his young face I wondered how long he would last in today's competitive, global world. Maybe the Spanish knight's great spirit would lead him boldly forward to conquer the dragons of cold-hearted greed. Or maybe he would be a teacher or a professor, inspiring a new generation of students to go out into the world, armed with indomitable faith and courage, to challenge the drooling beasts of injustice, suffering, and poverty. Either way, his life would be well spent.

CHAPTER EIGHT

A Good Man is Hard to Find

Canada's ocean playground

A s I walked past the ocean of cars crouched in the parking lot outside the Sobeys store on Windsor Street, I began musing about the words "Canada's Ocean Playground" that appear in blue letters on the bottom of our license plates. I don't know who suggested this as the motto of the Province of Nova Scotia, but to me it reflects the way other Canadians think about us. To my mind the image of a playground is not conducive to fostering the idea that Nova Scotia is a dynamic economic entity that is striving to achieve parity with other less playful provinces. If Canadians from the wealthier provinces see us as a cute little place to spend a holiday rather than an area where they would like to earn their living, they will continue to behave as they historically have.

I think it's fair to liken the behavior of our federal government's economic policy makers to the very rich man who tithes 10% of his net earnings to his church, uses 25% for normal living expenses and then blows the remainder on selfish pursuits, feeling quite righteous because he has been munificent in his charity. When things get tough this same man begins his program of restraint by reducing his tithing. This is how it is with regional funding. The majority of the voters are elsewhere, as is the economic force of the country, so self interest dictates that they be served first and well.

To continue the tithing analogy, Nova Scotia and the rest of Atlantic Canada are the charity recipients, so we must make do with the standard donation in good times and our usual cut backs in poor times. We are told that everyone must share in the policies of restraint. But we are not told that everyone will not share equally. I need not quote the statistics that show that per capita income is higher and unemployment lower in the province of Ontario than in Nova Scotia. If this is the case, then who can afford the cutback more easily? Who will be affected less? Since we didn't share equally in times of boom, why should we have to share equally in times of bust?

It's well known that the principal reason for failure among new business startups is lack of capitalization. I must admit that the federal government has invested a lot of money to assist Atlantic Canadians to build their economies. Unfortunately this is a marathon, not a sprint. In the case of my little company, it took eight years of capital reinvestment before Gordon was able to draw a modest salary (I continued to work for nothing for a sum total of 14 years).

One of the things to remember about equalization payments is that ultimately they're meant to fund self-help projects. This is just as well, for it's considerably easier and cheaper for Ontario to send us equalization payments than it is to see to it that we are truly equal. Hard words perhaps, but consider these facts: On the list of Canada's largest 500 companies, 40% of them are subsidiaries of foreign-owned companies, 55% have their headquarters in Ontario, 21% in Quebec, and 9% each in B.C. and Alberta. The other six provinces share the remaining six percent. Atlantic Canada has eleven companies from our four provinces on the list. Every one of these companies started here and has remained here. Not one listed company in the history of confederation has ever established its headquarters here if its origins were not here. The truth is, Atlantic Canada's four provinces are only pilot fish swimming under the great white sharks of Ontario and Quebec, hoping that enough crumbs will come their way to keep them alive. If we are ever going to get out from under we are going to have to make our own big fish.

So how do we go about doing this? Let me count the ways. First of all, the Atlantic Provinces should unite and behave like a school of piranhas to make sure that we get our fair share of help from Ottawa. Secondly, we should see to it that we support our local winners by trading with local companies as much as we possibly can. Harvey Webber, the Cape Bretoner who founded Atlantic Canada Plus, did his best to raise the consciousness of Eastern Canadians by reminding them over and over again to buy local products which, in turn, creates local employment. The time has come to get rid of the absurd notion that products are inherently better if they come "from away." And finally, we should change that wimpy motto on our license plates to read "Nova Scotia: Canada's Eastern Force."

A hare-brained marketing scheme

Gordon had been trying for some time to find a reliable right-hand man, one who could be trusted to handle everyday matters so that we could be free to grow the business. The search had been going on for years, but nobody ever seemed to fit the bill. Graduates from business schools invariably had "crown prince" complexes, thinking they deserved to sit on the throne merely because they had a post-graduate degree. People who did have experience in the real world were usually reluctant to get their hands dirty, so they were fairly useless when emergencies arose. The more qualified they were, the less work they did. They seemed to think that they had already paid their dues, and from then on they were entitled to put their feet up and watch the world go by.

For my own part, our frustrating search reminded me of my college days when my friends would complain that a good man was hard to find. In fact, there seemed to be an unwritten law saying that the harder you looked, the less likely you were to find him. All the girls seemed to know that their future mate would show up when they least expected it, but that was cold comfort to members of the "now" generation. Yet there was nothing any of us could do to get the law repealed. It stayed firmly on the books, and there it remains to this very day.

Gordon and I had no time to worry about unwritten laws. We were too busy running the business and putting out the usual "fires" that would erupt here and there with disconcerting frequency. On one such occasion our shelf stocker, or "merchandiser" in Halifax had decided to quit on the spur of the moment, so it fell to Gordon and me to jump into the car and drive to the city, where we were responsible for completing the work he had left undone. The job of a merchandiser involves going to the walk-in cooler in the back of a supermarket and stocking the store shelf with product, checking all the expiry dates that are stamped on the containers, and rotating the stock accordingly.

You would think that the stock boys who work at the stores would do this job, but that's not how it happens in the Maritime provinces. As I mentioned previously, this costly and inefficient system (from our point of view) came into being many years earlier, when someone in sales and marketing at one of the big three local dairies noticed that store clerks were often slow about restocking milk on the shelves. Large shipments of milk were in storage coolers in the back of the stores, but the shelves were often bare in the dairy cases where customers looked for the milk products. In order to address this problem, the dairy offered to send its own merchandisers to the supermarkets to see to it that "their" shelf space never had run-outs.

The chain stores, ever anxious to reduce their labor costs, loved the idea. Soon all dairies were told that they would have to provide equivalent service or their brand of products would be de-listed. We, being a dairy, were therefore required to send people to every supermarket that sold our yogurt to make sure that shelves were stocked with neatly arranged yogurt containers. It was obviously far more costly for us to provide this service than it was for the other dairies whose employees were in the stores every day stocking not only yogurt but also their companies' full line of corollary products such as fluid milk, cream, butter, ice cream, cheese, cottage cheese, fruit juice, and bottled water. Soon we had more employees working in the supermarkets than in all the rest of the company, including manufacturing, distribution, and administration. Our costs, of course, went through the ceiling, and we had no choice but to raise our prices to cover these exorbitant expenses.

So one little marketing guy with a hare-brained scheme managed in one fell swoop to boost the consumer price of Maritime dairy products to the highest level in Canada. This anonymous individual also opened another can of worms at the same time, for once the stores decided to let the dairies control the shelves, the situation got out of hand. Merchandisers from the various dairies, heady with their new freedom, jumped on the opportunity to move their competitors' products around to make more space for their own brand, thus creating a maelstrom of problems unseen by consumers but paid for by them as well. It was not unusual for merchandisers to steal shelf space, smash their competitors' products, and play dirty tricks that are too petty and too numerous to mention. All these unnecessary expenses had to be added to the price tag, especially since dairy products are sold to the chain stores on a guaranteed basis. This means that the dairy, not the supermarket, is responsible for product that is broken, returned, or that has exceeded its best-before date, so the retail prices reflect these hidden costs.

The unwritten law

It so happened, on that fateful day when Gordon and I set out for Halifax, that our erstwhile merchandiser had left all of his stores unattended. Since the day was already half over, we decided to divide up his stores between us in order to finish them on time. We agreed to meet at the lounge at the Sheraton Hotel at five o'clock to relax after our day's work. Gordon took the car and I got a cab, and off we went in our separate directions.

I dashed from store to store, running to the back cooler, wheeling the yogurt out to the dairy case on a cart, stocking the shelves, rotating the product, answering customer questions, then hurrying out again to the waiting taxi. As the afternoon progressed I could see that the driver, a young man with dark, curly hair and friendly blue eyes, was growing curious about my comings and goings.

"I don't think you're going to save any money with all this comparison shopping you're doing," he said at last.

After explaining to the taxi driver what I was really up to, I asked him if he knew anybody who would like to do the work I was doing that day. I would pay for the labor, gas, and mileage, but the candidate would have to own a car.

I waited quietly while the driver thought about my question. What a relief it would be if he could come up with a good, hard-working, reliable individual to do the job! If I could start training somebody the very next day, it would mean that I'd save myself at least three weeks of having to do the Halifax stores myself (a week for the ads to appear in the newspapers, a week for the candidates to reply, and a week for the interviews).

"I know someone who'd be great for the job," said the taxi driver. My heart leaped. "He's the best worker you'll ever meet, and *smart*! He's friendly, organized, responsible – a terrific guy!"

"He sounds perfect! How do I meet him? Do you know his phone number?"

"I know his number, all right. It's the same as mine. He's my kid brother."

I could have kissed the back of the taxi driver's head. Any little brother who could earn the respect of his older brother had to be superlative, and any older brother willing to praise his kid brother was a man of character and therefore a man whose opinions I would take seriously.

"There's a problem, though," the driver added. My heart sank. "He's only sixteen."

"Well, does he have a driver's license and a car?"

"Yes to both questions."

"So... what's the problem, then?"

"Well, he has school, you know. But he could go before classes, and between classes, and after school, and after supper, and all day Saturday..."

I worried a little bit about the scheduling. The grocery managers in the stores were never happy about product being left in the back coolers for very long. The truck drivers would leave the yogurt stacked on a pallet in the cooler, then the merchandiser was expected to show up in a car as soon as possible thereafter and get it lined up on the dairy case shelves. Long delays between the product delivery and stocking the shelves were frowned upon, sometimes leading to showdowns and threats from grocery managers or dairy case boys who understandably wanted the back cooler to be as empty as possible and the store shelves to be as full as possible at all times. Merchandisers had to be available to do this work in a timely manner or there could be serious consequences. I knew the store managers were under a lot of pressure to keep things running smoothly, and they especially wanted the shelves to look nice for the customers, so it was important to find a merchandiser who was free to follow the delivery trucks as closely as possible.

"My brother would be great for the job," said the taxi driver, after I explained the problems of scheduling. "The guy's a regular tornado. He never stops! He could drive to the stores in his free periods between classes. No problem. And don't worry, he's a straight A student."

The driver's praise was so generous that I began to wonder if it was a cover-up of some kind. Maybe the younger brother was just out of reform school and couldn't

get a job. Maybe... no, I'd know as soon as I met him. And
I could always check his record and get references.

"Is he free at five o'clock this afternoon?"

"He sure is. Where can he meet you?"

"I'll be in the lounge at the Sheraton Hotel. It overlooks
the boardwalk and the waterfront. I think it's called the
Harbourview Lounge."

"He'll be there," said the driver, his eyes beaming in the
rearview mirror.

"By the way, what's your brother's name?" I asked him.

"His name's Blair. Blair Landry."

Special delivery

As we sipped our beer in the Sheraton lounge that afternoon,
Gordon was tentatively pleased to hear my story about
finding a replacement for the Halifax merchandiser – but he
wasn't about to get excited until he at least had a chance to
meet the boy. I, on the other hand, like to get excited first. I
can always deal with disappointment later, but I hate the idea
of cheating myself out of a little excitement just because it
might be in vain.

But vain it appeared to be, for just then I saw the taxi
driver walking toward us. He was alone and Blairless. No
doubt he had come to let us know that his brother was not
interested in the job after all, or didn't have as much time on
his hands as he thought, or his mother had put her foot down,
or his car wasn't up to the task... it could have been any
number of things. But it certainly looked as though I was
going to be doing the merchandising in Halifax for the next
few weeks.

"Hi," said the taxi driver, approaching our table. "Sorry
to interrupt you, but I just wanted to tell you that Blair is
waiting for you out in the lobby. They wouldn't let him in
here. He's under age, you know. But take your time. He's
not in a rush."

Blair was 16 years old when we hired him that afternoon, and he was 24 when he became our plant manager. He was everything his brother said he was, and considerably more. He was endlessly curious about every aspect of the process of making yogurt, and he delved with gusto into the challenging and often frustrating job of becoming intimately acquainted with bacterial behavior. He read books. He burned the midnight oil. We sent him to ice-cream school in Guelph. He kept records. He invented new ways of keeping track of time, temperatures, bacterial counts, production numbers, and work schedules. He went to Dalhousie and majored in statistics. He was everywhere at once, and never got tired of learning. As far as the breadth and depth of his interest was concerned, he was the best student I ever had.

Gordon and I knew we would have to keep him happy, and above all, we would have to maintain his interest at the highest possible level. We had learned from past experience that our small yogurt company often piqued the curiosity of highly intelligent young college graduates, who would join the "family" because they were ideologically attracted by what we stood for: excellence, value for money, real food, honest dealings, hard work, small-is-beautiful, community spirit, and so on. But once they learned every aspect of the job they would often become bored and move on. This was hard on us, but we understood. If they felt called to go on to bigger and better things, we wished them well and began the long process of seeking and training their replacements.

But the time had come for us to start thinking of finding a future replacement for ourselves. By the early '90s we felt quite sure that neither of our daughters would want to take over the business. Valerie, who was then 20 years old, had already graduated from Dalhousie with a BA in Comparative Religion, and had also completed her Master's degree in Biblical Studies from the Dallas Theological Seminary. She had her heart set on becoming a medical missionary, so she still had many years of medical school and a residency ahead

of her. Vicki, our youngest, had fallen in love with a fellow
student at Calvin College in Michigan, where she was
studying art. It didn't seem likely to us that she would give
up either the young man or her future career as an artist or
teacher to join the ranks of the yogurt moguls.

Both girls knew all too well the heartbreak of owning a
small business that was forever teetering on the brink of
some calamity or other. A person has to have a certain type
of risk-taking personality to be able to live fairly comfortably
with the constant threat of disaster. People do it, and they do
it sometimes with grace and even heroism, but I don't think
many venture into these nightmares voluntarily if they know
from the start what is in store for them. Gordon and I
managed to stumble into the business with our eyes closed,
and our naïveté kept us going until financial responsibilities
and a deep pride in our product forced us onward. But the
eyes of our children were not closed. They had enjoyed a
close-up view of the worrisome, precarious existence of two
well-meaning entrepreneurs, and although they loved us and
respected our achievements, they were not prepared to take
over where we left off.

Blair, however, had begun to enjoy the chaotic quality of
life at Peninsula Farm. He never knew quite what to expect
from one day to the next – there were always new problems
to solve, new fires to put out, and new areas to explore. It
was a precarious, zigzag existence that forced him to learn to
tack back and forth in a raging wind over a turbulent sea in a
tiny, jerry-rigged boat, and Blair was the sort of person who
didn't mind being at the helm. In fact, he seemed to get
genuine pleasure from studying the wind and the weather
and figuring out the best, most practical ways of solving the
problems that naturally beset a small craft caught in such
vexing circumstances.

A good man may indeed be hard to find, but I said a
little prayer of thanks that my encounter with the taxi driver
that day was not quite as random as I had originally thought.

CHAPTER NINE

Daisy Goes Overseas

Bells Toll at the World Food Show

Once I had resigned from Dalhousie University and Gordon had me all to himself, he was determined to make Peninsula Farm a force to be reckoned with. Both our girls were now busy with their own lives. Valerie was a medical student at Columbia University's College of Physicians and Surgeons, so she would have her nose to the grindstone for many years to come. Vicki was married and the mother of our grandson, Harrison, as well as the proud owner of *The Printer's Inc,* a small print shop in Grand Rapids, Michigan. All of the ducks were lined up in a nice, neat row. The sky was the limit.

Gordon and I knew that the food show to beat all food shows takes place in Cologne, Germany, every three years. When we checked the calendar we found, to our delight, that we were in a Food Show year. We were by then well into the '90s, and to us the last decade of the millennium seemed golden with promise. Blair had organized his work so well that we were able to invite him to come with us to Germany, a bonus that was greatly appreciated by a young man who had not yet set foot on European soil.

I was glad the three of us could travel together without having to worry unduly about the business collapsing in our absence. Just to be on the safe side, of course, we gave our contact number to our faithful office manager, Sylvia Booth, who, along with her trusty lieutenant, Cheryl Lohnes, had calmly and confidently seen us through our ups and downs for the past decade.

And so it was that the three of us – Gordon, Blair and I – traveled to Germany to attend the world famous food show. Our purpose was to expose ourselves to new ideas from every corner of the earth. Was there a fruit we hadn't heard of, or that hadn't yet been invented? Let's be the first to blend it with yogurt. Was there a process that contributed to a better end product? Let's study it, and see if it can be adapted to our manufacturing methods at Peninsula Farm. Was there an innovative way to package our yogurt to attract new customers? Let's check it out and try to imagine how some bright new containers would look on the supermarket shelves.

When we arrived at the location of the food show the following morning, we could hardly believe our eyes. There were acres and acres of food of every description spread out before us in a honeycomb of exhibition halls that seemed to go on forever. No wonder we had been issued a map at the registration table! Naturally enough this honeycomb was a beehive of activity. The hopeful vendors had gone to every conceivable length to dress up their booths in such a way as to attract the attention of the visitors strolling by.

A great deal of money had evidently been spent on these endeavors, and the results were not only very professional but sometimes humorous as well. My favorite booth had a table laden with smoked and pickled fish, with a family of comical-looking dummies sitting around it, staring hungrily at the beautiful display of toothsome seafood. One almost felt sorry for them for being mannequins, since they could never hope to enjoy the succulent tidbits laid out in front of them.

As I was musing about the significance of this poignant scene, one of the mannequins smiled and offered me a tiger shrimp on a toothpick. I almost jumped out of my skin, but I composed myself and quickly accepted the shrimp lest it end up in the appreciative mouth of some other passerby.

The symbolic meaning was replete with possibilities, which increased ominously with each chew. I tried not to dwell too long on the vision of fat capitalists gorging on food that was provided at great human expense by workers living in less fortunate areas of the world. Perhaps the shrimp had been farmed, then mechanically shelled and deveined by machines that saved people the onerous task of harvesting and processing them by hand. But were the workers being adequately paid for their labor? Was the competition from farmed, mechanically-processed shrimp knocking harvested, hand-processed shrimp out of the market? Was there, perhaps, a good rationale for hanging on to wild shrimp and other fish?

I had heard some disturbing stories about how farmed fish lived in such crowded conditions that they needed to be fed antibiotics to keep them from dying of disease. I had also heard reports of how they were given food that was largely made up of ground fish with high mercury levels or containing other toxins that had been deemed unfit for human consumption. These poisons were merely entering our bodies through another doorway.

Some people would argue, however, that the shrimp factory approach was providing work at salaries higher than the usual level of pay in various areas of the globe, but how stable were the jobs? And how wise was it for workers in less-developed countries to put themselves into the hands of foreign interests? Did they have any choice?

To be sure, many people who never dreamed of owning a TV or a microwave were taking these items for granted now, but at what price? These economic practices had been going on for a long time. Perhaps, depending on how you defined exploitation, they had existed since the beginning of human history. The rich and the powerful have known from time immemorial how to defend their own interests.

As I walked along the aisles of the exhibition hall and viewed the amazing abundance and variety of foodstuff on display, I wondered if this economic process was beginning to accelerate, perhaps even at an alarming rate. Many would argue that it is to everyone's benefit when prices can be driven down by technological advances and better economies of scale, but what happens when small companies are driven out of business by prices that are too low for them to match?

No problem, say the pundits. The smaller companies need to be replaced by larger, more efficient corporations. It's the survival of the fittest. That's how it works in nature and on every level of human endeavor as well. As I glanced again at the surcease of food on display, I couldn't help asking myself for whom the bell tolled.

Instead of cocking an ear for tolling bells, the three of us moved through the showrooms, trying this, testing that, until the embarrassment of riches began to exercise an undesirable affect on my digestive system. Blair, on the other hand, blessed with the stainless steel gut of a young person, was unaffected by the eclectic nature of this approach to our daily sustenance. He stopped to chat with the salespeople at any booth whose food samples seemed even remotely associated with the production of yogurt, and a lively conversation would generally ensue.

By the end of the week we had gathered information on where to buy the best fruit from growers all around the world. What surprised us, however, was the fact that the price of fruit had more or less doubled since we had started our business 15 years earlier. What had happened to the vaunted prices that were supposed to be lowered due to improved technology and better economies of scale? We all know the concept of built-in obsolescence. Did these apparently needless price increases have something to do, perhaps, with built-in greed? Did the prices go up simply because it was within the purview of the powers-that-be to *make* them go up?

We were taken aback when a German broker offered us blueberries from our own supplier/grower in Nova Scotia at a lower price than we were paying him ourselves. How could berries grown in Nova Scotia, then shipped to Germany, then shipped back to Nova Scotia cost less than they were costing us to buy them directly from the Nova Scotian grower?

Later, when we returned to Canada, we made it a point to ask our supplier this question. We received a complex and unabashedly spurious explanation of international trade policies that produce high-volume orders and payments in currencies stronger than the Canadian dollar. After this conversation, however, our supplier found a way to give us a lower price on our blueberries over the following year, in an amount sufficient to cover most of our expenses for the trip to Cologne.

But why did we have to go all the way to Germany to find out that our own government supports large foreign businesses with Canadian commodities that are priced lower than they are at home? It made us very nervous indeed to discover that our elected officials are prepared to support foreign interests at the expense of local Canadian businesses, especially small ones. The bell tolled ominously.

The company motto

This was not the only price we had to pay for being small. It was impossible, for example, for us to avoid the extra cost of paying a broker to supply us with fruit, for the minimum size of a direct shipment was a full trailer load, or about 40,000 pounds. Although we processed approximately this amount of strawberries, blueberries, and raspberries every year, we couldn't afford to pay for this much fruit up front, so we had to buy from brokers at a considerably higher price. We looked back on the old days with a touch of nostalgia, for there was a time years ago when we did, in fact, buy a year's worth of fruit at the time of the pick, keeping it in frozen storage and using it as needed.

Owning so much fruit and storing it all in one place had its risks, however. A frozen storage building fell down on 25,000 pounds of our raspberries during a blizzard one year, but in those days we had enough of a financial cushion to survive a disaster of that magnitude. Now it was no longer quite so easy to compete with the giants when it came to economies of scale. We had learned through long experience that the only way to compete successfully with companies that were literally thousands of times larger than ours was to make a product that was undeniably better than theirs. This concept eventually became Peninsula Farm's motto: *"If you have to be the smallest, then you'd better be the best."*

Our company motto meant little or nothing, however, to the buyers at the supermarkets, because quality was never of great concern to them. They were interested only in price, rebates, deals, advertising, and marketing ploys. Over the years the various buyers in our category admitted to us that they either hated yogurt, or had never tasted it, or they disliked even the sound of the name itself. Fortunately for us we had a rather large base of loyal customers who disagreed with the buyers' opinion of yogurt, and their votes kept us in business in spite of it all.

It often occurred to me that our company motto applied not only to our small province but to all of Canada too, in its capacity as a small nation pitted against such giants as the European community and our good neighbor to the south. I used to make this observation when I addressed Canadian business groups both inside and outside the province, but I don't believe my ideas on this matter made much difference. Although my comments about Peninsula Farm's motto were always received with smiles and applause, I never noticed any businesses dedicating themselves whole-heartedly to the notion of being the best.

Excellence has been given a great deal of lip service, but when it comes to making a decision about costs, the bottom line wins every time. Our huge competitors are so keen to turn a profit on their yogurt that they have all but eliminated fruit from the product (while at the same time enhancing the colorful artwork depicting fruit on the containers). They have replaced real fruit with "aromas" or "natural flavor" essences, and have subsequently spent large sums of money marketing the yogurt as a superior product because it no longer contains any "lumps." This would be laughable were it not for the fact that people fall for it hook, line, and sinker. In those halcyon days of the '90s, however, we were still of the opinion that an excellent product could win the day.

With these thoughts in mind, we meandered through the halls and down the aisles of the exhibition grounds of the admirable food event taking place in Cologne. We were only half aware that the days of real food were numbered, and that healthy, natural products were slowly being replaced with ersatz food (not to mention the genetically-engineered products of the future) that was marketed as the real thing.

If we had stopped to think about the subject more deeply at that time, we might have been tempted to rejoice, knowing that the growing plethora of phony phood would make our product all the more rare and desirable. This might have been the case if all things had been equal and we had been playing on the much-vaunted "level playing field." But such things rarely happen in real life. Playgrounds are generally tipped in favor of the school bullies, and bullies learn from an early age that muscle and devious tactics win the day.

The vendors in the halls of the food show, however, had many delicious products for potential buyers to sample (what they did with these during the manufacturing process is another story). It was a joy to wander past the display booths, imagining how our yogurt might taste with the addition of ingredients that showcased the inimitable flavor of nature's own.

One of our most exciting discoveries was a lemon curd made by a British company and based on the original recipe of the woman who had founded the firm long ago. That lemon curd was to die for, and much to our great delight the salesman assured us that his company could sent it to us at a price we could afford.

"It's a shame to mix the lemon curd into the yogurt," Blair said that night during our usual wrap-up conference. "Wouldn't it be terrific if we could keep the two of them completely separate, so the customers could enjoy both the yogurt *and* the lemon curd? It's such great stuff!"

"You mean like fruit on the bottom?" Gordon asked.

"No, I mean like fruit on the top," Blair replied. "When it's on the bottom you can't really get at it without disturbing the yogurt and basically mixing them both together whether you want to or not."

"So you're talking about a sundae, then," I said.

"Yes, but technically I don't see how it can be done," Blair admitted. "If you set up the yogurt and it's warm, the fruit will sink to the bottom. If the yogurt's cold, that's fine, but there's no way to add the lemon curd afterwards without opening every container again, and that's insane, of course. I guess there's no way to solve this one. But what a shame! We go to all this trouble to find the best fruit in the world, and then we hide it under a bushel of yogurt. Not that there's anything wrong with the yogurt," he added hastily. "But it's the same problem with the yogurt, too. It's so good it should be eaten all by itself. But I don't know what the solution is. I wish I did!"

The answer presented itself the very next day in the hall where all the latest advances in dairy equipment were on display. There, sitting prominently in the middle of the hall, was a shiny stainless steel filling machine manufactured by the Grunwald company in Germany. An executive of the firm, Herr Anton Alt, stood proudly next to his machine, holding a small plastic container in his hand. The container had two sections in it – one to hold plain yogurt, and the other, smaller section, to hold the fruit portion. After peeling off the foil lid, the customer could bend the plastic between the two sections and tip the fruit onto the yogurt, thus creating a sundae-style treat. Voilà! End of problem.

Blair was over the moon. If we bought the Grunwald filling machine (at the rock-bottom price of $300,000.00), we would be the first food manufacturer in Canada to use the dual package container. Yogurt manufacturers in Europe had already switched over to the dual package system, and yogurt sales were higher than ever, according to Herr Alt.

"But don't take my word for it," he said. "I urge you to visit the yogurt pavilion as soon as possible. It is of utmost importance that you talk to the experts to hear their opinion."

Our sister city in Germany

It suddenly occurred to us that we might run across our old friend, Juergen Hagenow, in the yogurt pavilion. We had first met him about ten years before on a previous trip to Europe when we had purchased our first filling machine from the Trepko company in Denmark. We had finished our business ahead of time, so Gordon and I and our two young daughters found ourselves with a few days to spare. We had rented a car and were searching for a special destination.

"Here's one!" Vicki exclaimed, pointing to a particular spot on the map. "It's called *Lüneburg*, and it's in Germany. And look! They've spelled it wrong!"

We were all fascinated by her discovery of a little town whose name was almost exactly the same as *Lunenburg*, the village in Nova Scotia where we had lived for the last twenty years. We set out the very next morning for Lüneburg. It turned out to be one of the cutest little towns we had ever seen. Narrow, winding streets, brick houses with heavy beams and overhanging upper stories, and window boxes bursting with colorful flowers. A fairy story town!

Gordon made straight for the rat haus and asked to speak to the burgermeister. The girls hung back, mortified.

"Why does Dad talk about yogurt all the time to people he doesn't even know?" Vicki whispered to Val.

"It's called *schmoozing,*" she explained. "You have to do it if you want your business to grow."

"I don't understand how you can get anything done by snoozing," Vicki said, looking dubious. "Anyway, how can Dad expect the *mayor* to come out and talk to him?"

But that is exactly what he did. We were greeted by a tall, balding man in his early forties wearing gray trousers and a dark blue, hand-knitted vest. To our great surprise he knew all about Lunenburg, Nova Scotia. He informed us that many years ago there had been considerable fanfare about our being sister cities. Some friendly correspondence and even some celebratory visits had been exchanged, and now here we were, the new delegates from Lunenburg on an informal inspection tour!

The burgermeister was an outgoing, intelligent man who greatly pleased Vicki and Valerie by having his assistant serve them cookies and hot chocolate on a silver tray.

"So you run a yogurt business," he said, as we sipped our coffee. "Is that because of us?"

We stared at him and blinked.

"I'm afraid we don't understand," I said, finally.

"We have a famous yogurt company here in Lüneburg. We ship yogurt all over the country. I thought perhaps you wanted to carry on our tradition in the New World."

Gordon boldly asked if we could have a tour of their yogurt plant. The good mayor immediately picked up the phone and asked the plant manager to accommodate us, insinuating that we had come all the way from Canada just to inspect his factory.

And that is how we met Juergen Hagenow, an intense, hard-working man who was genuinely pleased to have the opportunity to talk about yogurt with two appreciative and knowledgeable visitors. Val and Vicki looked heavenward.

To our great surprise, the Lünebest yogurt plant looked much like our own, but with more square footage. Juergen's pasteurization vats were of a similar size, but he had three times the number. His incubator room had been built by his own employees, and the size had increased as production volumes warranted. His floor was cracked and pitted from moving heavy equipment and from continuous washing with strong cleaning agents. But it was a plant that meant business. It produced enough yogurt to satisfy customers all over Germany.

"If I spent my money making this place look like the Ritz Carleton, I'd soon be out of business," Juergen stated in answer to my inquiries about the necessity of keeping everything looking bright and shiny. "I'm not interested in cosmetics. I'm interested only in doing the job right. My yogurt gets tested every day. If the bacterial counts get too high, I find out why and I look for a solution. Usually it's a simple one. I refuse to spend anything at all on unnecessary changes. It's just money down the drain, and in this business every *pfennig* counts."

"That's a funny way to say *penny*," Vicki whispered.

We learned a lot from Juergen that afternoon. He gave us the idea of putting electric household fans in the incubator room to circulate the warm air evenly around the pallets of yogurt so that they would all set up properly and at the same time. He also suggested that we take our milk 20 degrees Celsius above the normal pasteurization level to deactivate the enzymes, as they often interfered with the bacterial action during incubation.

"One last word of advice," Juergen said as he led us and our relieved children out of the yogurt factory. "Get rid of as many employees as you can. It's much cheaper to care for a machine than it is to pay a human being to do the same work. Machines never complain, you know, and they don't go on strike, either."

Fortunately Juergen never mentioned anything about this topic when we introduced him to Blair at the food show in Cologne, almost two decades after our first meeting in Germany. We told him we had decided to buy the Grunwald filling machine and the dual package system, a decision which Juergen endorsed without hesitation. It was the system of choice throughout Europe, he assured us, and he congratulated us on being the first to introduce it to Canada. So after a delightful, informative and sometimes nostalgic conversation over lunch with Juergen in the German pavilion, we said our goodbyes and readied ourselves for our flight back to Nova Scotia.

The new filling machine had cost a small fortune, but it was worth the risk, we decided, just for the pleasure of seeing our customers enjoying creamy yogurt and home-cooked fruit presented sundae-style in the new dual pack containers. We were looking forward to the day when our brand new filling machine would come heaving over the brow of the hill on the edge of our farm in Lunenburg. Soon it would be humming away in our factory, and life would be better than ever.

We had turned a decidedly deaf ear to any bells that might have been making a half-hearted attempt to toll faintly somewhere in the distance.

CHAPTER TEN

Our Tenuous Leap Forward

Filling the plant with filling machines

The production crew at Peninsula Farm awaited the arrival of the Grunwald filling machine with great anticipation. With two filling machines in operation at the same time, they reasoned, their working hours would be sharply reduced. Since we had put them all on salary instead of paying them by the hour (this evened out seasonal fluctuations), they found this scenario profoundly appealing.

Gordon tried to disabuse them of their notion as gently as possible. Our purpose in expending such a huge sum of money on a new filling machine had not been primarily to save them labor hours at the same salary, but rather to increase production and therefore profitability. The length of the work day would remain the same, although the nature of their work would no doubt be somewhat modified.

"I hope we don't have as much trouble with this filling machine as we had with the Trepko machine," said Michelle, a cheerfully pessimistic young woman who had been with us since her late teens.

She was referring to our first filling machine, a huge L-shaped stainless steel monster that thoroughly dominated the rest of our equipment, both in complexity and sheer heft. Gordon and I had whisked the girls off to Denmark, where we examined the machine at the manufacturer's factory.

It was the smallest filling machine on the Trepko factory floor, and it looked very modest in size and appearance when we saw it standing among its more imposing companions.

But as soon as it arrived in Lunenburg, we knew we were in trouble. The fact that the machine was L-shaped presented a major difficulty. How would we get it through the door? We briefly contemplated the idea of removing the roof and lowering it into place with a crane, but we discarded this notion as being altogether too daunting. There had to be an easier way. The only other option was to disassemble the machine, wheel it through the door, and put it together again.

It turned out not to be very difficult to take it apart, but as every amateur tinkerer knows, putting a complicated piece of equipment together again was another story entirely. When we tried to operate the poor Trepko filling machine we discovered that all the timing was wrong. The cup dispenser was out of sync with the lidder, the pump squirted yogurt between the holes where the cups were supposed to be, and warning lights were flashing hysterically all over the place. Would we have to bring a mechanical engineer all the way from Denmark to unravel this mess? We shuddered at the very thought of what it would cost.

We were blessed beyond measure to be living in a place like Lunenburg, where for generations the residents had been self-sufficient and knew how to fix anything under the sun without having to depend on outside help. We had access to a blacksmith, machinists, welders, and talented men of all kinds who felt at home with equipment of any size, shape, or description. Gordon happened to know a man of this type who had lived in Lunenburg all his life and who was probably a genius when it came to mechanical ability.

Leonard Stevens showed up right away when Gordon called him. He studied the wiring diagram for a little while, and within a few hours he had the Trepko filling machine humming along contentedly. It filled the cups with just the right amount of water during the test run, and slapped the lids down on the cups with all the precision the Danish designer had originally intended. Gordon looked on in awe and gratitude while the moving parts performed their routine in perfect harmony.

Leonard accepted his payment willingly enough, but when we tried to praise him on his extraordinary mechanical skills and engineering abilities, he received the compliments with a dismissive wave of the hand and a self-deprecatory grunt. Such are the men of Lunenburg County.

Now, when the Grunwald filling machine heaved its way over the horizon, Gordon took one look at it and knew we were in for more trouble. It was crated so well that it could have easily withstood an attack from a Sherman tank. What's more, the crating added so much bulk to the overall size of the machine that it quickly became apparent that it would have to be uncrated outside the factory. This meant that it would be unprotected when the time came to lift it up onto the loading dock, thus exposing it to the possibility of toppling over during this crucial procedure.

"I guess I'll have to call a man," said Gordon, with a conspiratorial wink.

I knew he was referring to my widowed mother's oft-stated comment about "calling a man" whenever something needed to be done that was outside her purview. She had belonged to a generation of women who were not expected to be handy around the house, but this never proved to be a problem for her. She never hesitated to "call a man" at the least provocation, and they were always willing to oblige.

We all stood around with bated breath while a man from Lunenburg slowly raised the Grunwald filling machine, perched precariously on the extended tines of a forklift, over the platform of the loading dock. Three hundred thousand dollars teetered in the balance. It was like taking a chance with a brand new house. Then a shout of triumph arose from our production crew as the man gently lowered the machine onto the pallet jacks situated on the dock. Once again a man from Lunenburg had prevailed, and again he dismissed his feat as something beneath consideration.

"Ain't nothin' to it," he said with a shrug. "I know twenty lads can do that there sort of thing."

Lest anyone think we were ill-advised to spend what to us was a vast amount of money on a filling machine whose main purpose was to deal with a specialized dual package, let me just mention that the machine also came equipped with a heat-sealer that could slap foils onto our other line of yogurt containers as well. This was a great boon to us, as it allowed us to do away with our expensive plastic lids on the smaller containers, while at the same time it answered the customer desire for tamper-proof packaging. Now it remained for me to work out some recipes and a name for our brand new line of yogurt.

Tip-a-Topping

After much thought and consultation with our employees, I finally came up with the idea of calling the new line *Tip-a-Topping.* This seemed to satisfy everyone. Then, after a year's worth of research and development (most of which preceded the delivery of the filling machine), followed by extensive taste-tests based on a variety of possible toppings, I finally settled on five basic flavours. They were *chocolate,* made with pure cocoa and bricks of Dutch chocolate; *lemon,* made with a lemon curd manufactured in Great Britain; *raspberry,* made with a seedless *coulis* we produced ourselves with fresh frozen raspberries; as well as *strawberry* and *blueberry,* based on the fruit processed in our own plant using fresh frozen product.

It now remained for me to sell our new Tip-a-Topping line. The buyers at the two supermarket chains had grown used to the fact that our company was now a permanent fixture on the business landscape, so they allowed me to list the new line as long as I placed it in my own shelf-space. No problem. I had no intention of invading my competitors' space, especially since I knew full well that such a move would lead to World War III.

Weeks went by, and nothing happened. Although my friends assured me that it was the best dairy product they had ever tasted, our new line of yogurt nevertheless sat on the shelves until it expired and had to be replaced.

"I can't understand why Tip-a-Topping isn't moving," I said to Gordon one morning.

"I think the price is too high."

"But I've figured out our costs very carefully. How can we survive if we sell it below cost? Besides, keeping the ingredients separate allows us to showcase the incredible deliciousness of both the yogurt and the fruit. It has to be obvious to everybody that it's a superior product and that we're asking a fair price for something that undeniably has knock-your-socks-off quality."

"Yes, well people aren't willing to pay extra to have their socks knocked off," Gordon remarked.

"What? Why not?" I asked indignantly.

"It's like everything else," he said wearily. "People want something for nothing. Everybody wants a bargain."

"But you get what you pay for!"

"Exactly. And that's why the other yogurt producers have nothing to worry about. They'll always have customers because their yogurt is cheap. What it tastes like is not all that important as far as most people are concerned."

"Why does anyone ever buy a Mercedes, then? Why don't they just settle for some cheap car if all they want to do is get from A to B?"

"I guess because when you buy a Mercedes, everybody sees you behind the wheel. You're telling the world you have money and status. But when you buy Peninsula Farm yogurt, you eat it at home where nobody sees you. What good is that to someone who wants to impress his neighbor?"

"Then why are we still in business? Why do we succeed at all?"

"Because there are always people who will buy an item for its intrinsic quality, and not just to impress others."

"But do you think there are enough of them to pay for the filling machine?"

"That's up to you," Gordon said, with an encouraging little pat on the back. "You're not only in charge of R&D, but you've got marketing and sales on your plate, too."

"I've never been much good at selling, though," I said morosely. "I've always hoped they'd sort of beat a path to my door."

"There's more to it than that, I'm afraid. You've got to make the best product first of all, and then you have to get it out there, and not only that, people have to know it's there. So if you can do that, and I know you can, then I promise you that Blair and I will see to it that it gets made properly, and we'll get it to the stores on time as well."

I set my mind on selling Tip-a-Topping with a fresh sense of purpose and renewed determination. I would do non-stop "demos" in all the stores throughout the Maritime Provinces. We had already established an excellent track record with these in-store demonstrations, which gave us a wonderful opportunity to communicate with our customers. I'd wheedle, cajole, explain, hand out pamphlets, and give away free samples till the cows came home. I would surely prevail in the long run. People would taste my samples and conclude that life isn't worth living without Tip-a-Topping. Excellence is addictive. Enthusiasm is contagious. Victory would be certain.

No more demos

It took me two weeks to work out the scheduling, logistics, and expenses involved in visiting over 200 stores in three provinces. When I finally had my plan in place, I called up the head offices of the two supermarket chains to make the usual arrangements. To my utter bewilderment the buyers in both chains informed me that they were no longer allowing suppliers to do their own demos. They preferred to have "professional" demonstrators hand out samples of all the products sold in the stores.

"A professional demonstrator?" I said. "What's *that*?"

"We've contracted a public relations firm to send their own demonstrators to the stores," one of the buyers told me. "They're all going to have the same uniforms and the same demonstration booths."

"But there's one little problem here. The demonstrators won't know anything about yogurt!"

"Yes, they will," the chain store buyer said firmly. "The PR company is going to take care of their training. They'll be taught nutrition, and they'll know everything about the food values of all the products they demo."

"That's absurd!" I exclaimed, feeling the blood rush to my face. "Knowing the food values isn't enough! It would take weeks for demonstrators to absorb all the information there is to know about yogurt, to the point where they can confidently answer any question the customer might have. But these people are going to be expected to demo yogurt one week, and smoked salmon the next, and who knows what after that? They'll never be able to learn enough about yogurt. And besides, what do PR guys know about it? I'll bet you they don't even eat it themselves. So what's so professional about all this?"

"The PR company knows how to sell," said the buyer, forcing himself to be patient. "They're professionals at selling products. Any product. Besides, it will *look* more professional, too. The uniforms and the booths are going to be designed with the store colors and logos. It'll all be one package. It's what we want for our image."

"So if I want you to demo my yogurt, what do I do?"

"You get in touch with me, I arrange a schedule, and you pay me in advance."

To my distress I learned that I'd have to pay the head offices a sum of money that was greater than what it cost me to do my own demos, and even then I'd have an unknown person, trained by some anonymous yogurt "expert," talking about my product. But she would *look* professional, no doubt about that. She would be just another pretty package, like all the other packages on the shelves. Even if I wanted to take the trouble to train her, there was no guarantee the PR company would let me do it, and there was also no way to be sure they wouldn't assign a different person to do the demo every time. And who would stop her from using my training and information to promote my competitors' yogurt? The whole situation was obviously absurd, but the head office was going to make a tidy profit at those prices. It would all seem to be so very professional, so pretty, so color-coded, so empty, so infuriating!

"Maybe I can go work for the PR company, and demo my own yogurt through them," I said to the buyer.

"Maybe so, who knows? But you don't exactly look like a demonstrator."

"Really? What does a demonstrator look like?"

"I don't know."

"Then how do you know I don't look like one?"

My question got me exactly nowhere, except into the bad graces of the buyer. When would I ever learn?

I felt greatly troubled that from then on an unknown yogurt demonstrator would be controlling the information that was presented to my customers. How could I ever tell them the truth about yogurt? How would I ever again distinguish my own product from all the others? I was now very effectively muzzled, and this, of course, was just what my competitors wanted. I wondered which one of them had cooked up this latest scheme to cut me off and shut me up.

I was worried and upset by all of this, especially since Gordon and I had always increased our sales dramatically in the past after completing a whirlwind tour of demos in our 200 stores. But now we were no longer permitted to interface with the public in our own demo booths (which, by the way, looked very professional and had cost us a considerable sum of money that was now down the tubes). There was nothing for it but to seek new markets to increase our sales to meet our ever-spiraling costs.

CHAPTER ELEVEN

Daisy Explores the World

Trade mission to Puerto Rico

When I got home I told Gordon how annoyed I felt about the whole concept of professionalism in general and my competitors' modus operandi in particular. There wasn't a package of anything in the stores that wasn't presented with beautiful color photographs of the products inside, but you would invariably have a hard time recognizing what it was you were looking at when you got it home and opened the box. Didn't anybody care? Why did they buy this ersatz food? Why didn't people demand *real* food?

"I thought you'd be interested in this," Gordon said, after my last grumble finally disappeared into the ether. He handed me a letter.

"What is this?" I asked, without much enthusiasm.

"How would you like to go on a trade mission to Puerto Rico?"

At first the idea didn't appeal to me at all. It seemed like a long way to send a container of yogurt. I thought ruefully of the day when I happened to be at the airport and I saw a pallet of our yogurt sitting unprotected on the tarmac on a hot summer day, waiting to be loaded into the hold of a cargo plane heading for Newfoundland.

"I don't need the aggravation," I said, wearily.

But Gordon managed to get me to change my mind by convincing me I had nothing to lose and maybe some little piece of unexpected market share to gain. If 80% of Nova Scotian yogurt consumers preferred to buy yogurt from "away" on the ill-conceived notion that imported foods are always superior to products made at home, then it stood to reason that there might be Puerto Ricans who would stand in line to get their hands on a nice, frosty dairy treat made in the frozen north. Perhaps it might hold the exotic appeal of being a product from "away" as far as they were concerned.

"Any Puerto Rican public relations company could do miracles with the idea," Gordon said with a wink. "Yogurt from Canada, the land of igloos and polar bears, where ice-cold dairy products abound."

"A PR PR firm," I smiled.

"What?"

"A Puerto Rican Public Relations firm. I'll try to dig one up while I'm down there. I might as well fight fire with fire. What else can I do?"

"Watch it. Your values are slipping. Next thing you know you'll have our whole company going professional."

Two weeks later I found myself in a nondescript hotel room in downtown San Juan, surrounded by construction gangs and the perpetual sound of jack hammers. A thin layer of cement dust covered every surface in my hotel room, including my tongue and throat. All the more reason to go out early every morning in search of buyers for my yogurt.

The purchasing managers at the supermarket chains in Puerto Rico were much more respectful and polite than their counterparts in Nova Scotia. Perhaps they were not used to conversing in their own language with a woman whose business card indicated that she was a PhD and the CEO of her own company. Or maybe it was just another example of being considered important or special because I was "from away." At any rate, I had some very fruitful talks with the head office buyers who were not only willing to taste the samples I had brought with me, but were enthusiastic about carrying my product in their stores.

No rebates or listing fees were even discussed. The buyers seemed completely relaxed about the idea of giving the product a try, and if it did well we'd discuss a division of profits when we knew what the numbers were. I began to think there might actually be hope for a little company like ours on this congenial island.

"How are other refrigerated products shipped down here from off-shore?" I asked José Pacheco, a knowledgeable wholesaler who specialized in imported foods.

"We usually fly them in from Texas and Florida," he said. "But your yogurt isn't valuable enough to ship it that way. It only works for expensive items like shrimp, for example, or lobster. It has to have a certain price per pound before you can consider air freight as a possible option."

"What about shipping it by sea?"

"You have a shipping company in Nova Scotia called Irving. It is located in a province called New Brunswick. You must know about this Irving, yes?"

I certainly did.

"Irving has container ships that come down here on a regular basis," he continued. "It takes them five, maybe six days to get here from up there where you live. This is because they have to stop in New York and perhaps Miami first. They have refrigerated containers, but they charge you more for partial loads. I think you will have no problem, though. You will soon be able to fill a whole container when our people become fans of your yogurt."

Things were looking up. I was beginning to feel one or two rays of tentative hope. But there were a number of other hurdles to get over before I could look seriously at Puerto Rico as a market. For one thing, I would have to find a distributor. Brokers don't usually act in that capacity, but José suggested that I contact a company that was considered the number one fish distributor on the island.

"Unfortunately fish and yogurt don't make very good bedfellows," I pointed out. "The slightest hint of a fishy

odor emanating from a pallet of yogurt would put an abrupt
end to everything for me, although it would be no skin off
the nose of the fish distributor."

"Skin off the nose?"

"It would be no problem for him to ship the fish with the
yogurt, but it would be a very big problem for me to ship my
yogurt with his fish."

"Ah yes, I see. Well, how about fresh vegetables, then?"
José suggested. "Vegetables are cleaner than fish. The yogurt
would travel well with them. I can put you together with the
best distributor."

"That wouldn't work well either, I'm afraid. Veggies
don't need to be kept as cold as yogurt, and if your man is
smart he's not going to want to waste power by keeping the
temperature lower than necessary for the sake of the yogurt."

"What about meat, then?"

"I hate to be negative, but meat is bloody. If there were
the slightest leak in the packaging, it could drip on my load.
I've been through that already, and it wasn't pretty."

"I don't know how to help you, then," José said sadly.
"I would very much like to be the broker for your yogurt, but
this distribution problem is a puzzle to me."

"Dairy products go best with other dairy products, I
think. Which is the best dairy on the island, would you say?"

"Alpine. No question about it."

"Well, do you think they'd be interested?"

"I am not sure if they want to help a competitor, but who
knows? You might be able to help them, too. It is worth a
try. I will give you their phone number and you can try to
talk to them about this. Tell them you are here on a Canadian
trade mission. They will receive you."

They "received" me that very afternoon. I conversed in
Spanish with the general manager and the distribution
manager, both of whom were friendly and intelligent men
who knew the dairy business very well. They immediately
saw the possibility of our working together, because when
we sat down and tasted samples of our respective products it

was evident that theirs was developed with low consumer prices in mind, whereas mine was positioned at the high end of the market. We agreed that we could cover both ends of the market without stealing sales from each other.

When I asked the general manager to let me take a look at his storage cooler, though, my enthusiasm began to wane. I could see immediately that the "best before" dates on the dairy products were jumbled together in sad disarray. There seemed to be no system for storing the products with the oldest dates closest to the loading dock, so they would be the first to be delivered when the trucks left the dock.

I found this worrisome. I had already suffered through situations where various distributors allowed my yogurt to expire in their own storage coolers because of poor or non-existent inventory and stock rotation systems. In these cases I, of course, was always charged for the expired product on the grounds that it "didn't sell" or that it "spoiled."

I would have dearly loved to insist that the distributor be responsible for the expired yogurt since *he* was doing the ordering and the stock rotation, but I've never done business with anyone who showed even the slightest inclination to take responsibility for anything. Unfortunately there was very little I could do about such situations, for the distributor controls the payments that are remitted by the grocery stores selling the manufactured product.

I could always cut off relations with an unsatisfactory distributor, but most distributors are unsatisfactory anyway, and there aren't that many to choose from in any given geographical area. The alternative, owning my own fleet of trucks, is bad enough in the home territory but unthinkable in a region beyond one's immediate control.

The worst problem was that I was invariably the smallest player in any business deal, so naturally I ended up taking all the risks and paying all the costs. No wonder corporations want to get bigger and bigger. It's a Monopoly world. Once you get hotels on Boardwalk, you win the game.

The next day I grabbed a cab and went to half a dozen supermarkets, armed with my trusty pocket thermometer. To my infinite disappointment I found out that not one dairy case registered a temperature under 40 degrees Fahrenheit, and some were considerably higher. It was clear to me that my yogurt would never survive dairy case temperatures that hovered, on average, in the mid to high fifties.

All the other brands of yogurt contained preservatives to protect them from spoiling in these unsatisfactory conditions. The absence of real fruit also contributed to the long shelf-life, for fruit has a tendency to ferment when it gets too warm. This causes the lid on the yogurt container to bulge, and creates an off-flavor and an effervescence that is not dangerous to public health but is rarely appreciated by the discerning customer.

A facilitator to the rescue

By the end of the week I had abandoned all hope of taking on the market in Puerto Rico. I joined my associates on the trade mission for a goodbye cocktail party at the Canadian consul's house, feeling rather glum and a bit worried about what I could do to increase my sales.

The other businessmen on the mission, however, didn't seem to share my gloomy mood. In fact, they all looked relaxed and healthy, their skins glowing with brand new sun tans. They must have done most of their business research on the white sand beaches of this attractive island.

"Do I hear whining?" blurted a florid, rather bloated young man whom I had not seen before. He brashly joined our little group, introducing himself as Jonathan Blake, an experienced import/export broker specializing in Canadian products. He wanted us to know that he was at our service.

"You'll never get anywhere with all this negative talk," he said, looking in my direction. "Did I hear you say you're going home without closing even *one* deal?" he asked me.

I wanted to tell him it was none of his business, but I've lived in Canada long enough to have picked up the Canadian inability to be downright rude (unless, of course, you're a dairy case Nazi reveling in your undeserved power over harassed, frustrated, hard-working merchandisers).

"Look, I have connections all over the island," Blake said, sloshing some of his whisky sour onto his shoe. "I can introduce you to the right people."

"Thanks, but I've already met all the people I need to speak to. But I appreciate your interest."

"Well, how did it go?"

"It went fine."

"So did you make any deals?"

"No. It's not going to work out for me here."

"When are you going home?"

"Tomorrow," I said stiffly, trying to turn away. I noticed that nobody else in the group had deigned to answer.

"Tomorrow?" he guffawed. "You're giving up *already*? But you only just got here!"

"We've been here for a whole week," I told him. "And that's plenty of time for information-gathering."

"No, no, no, no," he said, vigorously shaking his head. "You don't understand. That's not how people do business down here. You can't get anywhere in just one week. What you do is you give it time. You socialize. You get cozy with people. You buy 'em a drink."

"It's not about socializing," I insisted. "It's about assembling the facts."

Why was I taking the bait? I saw my colleagues slipping away from the group, one by one.

"No. You're missing the point. You're missing the point completely. You can't come down here and get to know the whole culture in just one week. That's why you need *me*. I've lived here for three years now. Do you habla español? I bet you don't. That's where I can help you."

I was completely alone with the broker now.

"Hey, I'm going for another drink. The bar's right over there. It's free, you know. You might as well take advantage of it while you can. You want me to get you something?"

"No thanks. I'm fine," I said.

"Well, stay right there. I'll be back in a jiffy."

I was off like a shot.

Watch out! They're back again!

"You're absolutely right," said Gordon, chuckling at my story about the Canadian broker living in Puerto Rico. "No amount of socializing is going to improve the distributors' ordering system, or change their stock rotation system, or lower the temperature of the coolers in the stores."

"Oh, and I forgot to tell you, when I was out in the yard behind the dairy plant I noticed that not one of their trucks had a refrigeration unit. When I asked them how they kept their dairy products cool, they said the trucks had steel plates under the floor boards which they plugged in and froze every night. Apparently these plates keep the product pretty cool in the morning, but they admitted they defrosted by noon or so, and the cold had completely worn off by the time the trucks got back to the yard at the end of the day. So that would have been another problem for us if we had decided to go down there."

"It's just as well, then," said Gordon, resigning himself to the situation. "But it's a good thing you went and checked things out. It would have been disastrous for us if we'd lost a container load of yogurt because of any one of the potential problems you discovered. We can't afford that kind of loss."

"Tell me about it."

"So shall we try Toronto again?" said Gordon, eager to keep me on the road before I lost too much steam.

The last time we tried to penetrate the Toronto market we wanted to take advantage of the freight subsidies that were associated with hauling product out of the Maritime provinces. The cost of sending product to Ontario was quite attractive at the time, but we made the mistake of trying to negotiate with the chains so that we could ship enough product to make a full truck load, which was quite a bit less expensive than having the trucking company haul a partial load. The terms and conditions set forth by the chains were entirely too onerous for a small company like ours, however, so we had to abandon the idea of shipping our yogurt to Toronto.

Both Gordon and I felt disappointed when our plans fell through, but the idea of planning a future attack on Toronto had always remained at the back of our minds. Having two million customers all in one place seemed like an incredible luxury to us. We were used to sending our fleet of tractor-trailers all over the Maritimes, only to drop a relatively small amount of yogurt in the various stores. The cost of fuel alone was enough to daunt even the hardiest entrepreneur.

We decided it was time to try again. Our sales were flat in the Maritimes, and something had to be done. The freight subsidies had long since been abandoned, so there was no point in worrying about sending a full load with the trucking companies. But we had a small straight truck of our own that was only being used once a week, so with a few changes in the delivery schedule it wasn't difficult to liberate the truck to go to Toronto on a weekly basis.

The next step was for me to fly to Toronto and examine the market in much the same way I had done it in Puerto Rico. I visited every gourmet store individually, and had no trouble placing the product. Naturally the independent stores were pleased at the opportunity of carrying an item that was unavailable in the supermarkets. The rebates would be built in to the selling price, which was reflected in the high ticket price of all the products on the shelves. Apparently the kind of customer who shopped in the gourmet stores was used to the higher prices, and I was assured by all the owners that this would not affect the volume of sales.

I was also pleased to note that the temperature of the dairy cases was lower than 4 degrees Celsius in all the stores. The rest was in our hands. The truck driver, since he had fewer stops in Toronto, would have plenty of time to take inventory and calculate the amount of yogurt needed for the following week, so poor ordering would not be an issue. And since we'd be using our own truck with its excellent refrigeration unit, we'd have no problem keeping the product at the proper temperature at all times. Finally, the storage and rotation of the yogurt would be done correctly at the farm, so I could foresee no difficulties of the type that would have emerged in Puerto Rico.

It turned out that there was one thing I had not foreseen, however, and it was no small matter. By this time in our development our competitors were aware of our existence. They also kept a careful eye on what was happening on their home turf. So from the very moment Peninsula Farm yogurt appeared in the gourmet specialty stores, the other yogurt producers lowered their prices to a level that no customer could resist.

I immediately started a round of demos, enlisting the help of my daughter, Valerie, who happened to be on vacation at the time. She quickly hired and trained three more demonstrators to join the fray, and for several weeks we did our best to introduce our yogurt to as many taste buds as possible.

Valerie and her team did a superb job of demonstrating our yogurt, but in the end it turned out that their efforts were in vain. The product was unknown in Toronto, and although the customers who tasted the yogurt were impressed with it, they were still more impressed with the rock-bottom prices offered by our competitors. I couldn't help but feel flattered by the all-out effort the global companies made to keep us out of what they considered to be "their" territory, but it was a sad day for all of us at Peninsula Farm when we were finally obliged to fold up our tents and slip silently away.

Daisy down under

"Well, Blair and I kept the yogurt moving in and out of the stores while you were gone," said Gordon. "But it's good to have you home again."

"I'm glad to be back," I said. "But I hate being gone for so long with nothing to show for it. I feel miserable about that."

"Don't worry about it. Anyway, I have a surprise for you. We're going to Australia. I have it all arranged. Blair is doing great with production and distribution, and Cheryl has the merchandisers under control. Crystal is right on top of accounts payable, and Sylvia is the perfect office manager cum mother hen. So we're outta here!"

I felt my spirits lift for the first time in a long time, but *Australia!*

"Why Australia? What's happening there?" I asked.

"The 23rd International Dairy Conference is what. It's taking place in Melbourne this year, and they're requesting your presence."

"Right. I'm so sure!"

"It's true. We're both registered. They sent us a badge and a registration package, so now all we have to do is show up."

"Can we afford to go?"

"We can't afford not to, that's what I say. Delegates from all the biggest dairies on earth will be there, as well as buyers from major chains around the world. We're bound to learn something. We have to keep our ears to the ground. Maybe some little detail, some little snippet of conversation will spark an idea for turning this business around."

"We can both just leave together, at the same time, just like that, and the world won't come to an end?"

"Not if Blair and Sylvia and Crystal and Cheryl have anything to say about it. They're in charge now."

The one good thing to come out of my trip to Toronto, I thought to myself as we flew to Australia, is that everyone at Peninsula Farm seemed to have learned to get along just fine without me. Maybe I should modify that. After being away for so many weeks, I was the one who had learned I was not indispensable. Other people could be trusted to do their jobs properly as long as they had been well trained, had plenty of experience, and a proven track record.

I wasn't about to go so far as to say that entrepreneurs should learn to delegate authority to just anyone. I had lived long enough to realize that a good employee is hard to find, and in fact is almost always a diamond in the rough until he has been trained, polished, and has proven himself many times over. But when, towards the end of a lifetime of work and worry, an entrepreneur finds herself with a couple of diamonds on staff, then maybe, just maybe, she can afford to loosen her grip on the steering wheel. It feels good, I thought, as I pushed my seat back and settled myself in for the long journey to the other side of the world.

When we landed in Sydney we were met by my first cousin, Joan Van Gelder, and her husband John. She was my father's sister's daughter, and I had never seen her before in my life. I was surprised, however, that she didn't look familiar to me. She didn't resemble my father at all, or even my aunt, as far as I could tell. I had to assume that she took after her father's side of the family. But as the days wore on (she had been kind enough to invite us to stay with her for a week, sight unseen) and I got to know her better, I could see personality traits that reminded me of my sister, Heather. She was friendly, gregarious, and had a marvelous sense of humor. She also had the family talent for drawing and painting, some very competent examples of which were hanging on her walls.

But if Joan was unfamiliar to me, my mouth dropped open when her granddaughter, Vivian Van Gelder, stopped by for a visit. She looked for all the world like my daughter Vicki. The resemblance was uncanny. They were the same height, build, and age. They had the same dark hair, green eyes, and olive complexion. They even had the same full lower lip and shy smile. I couldn't help but stare, much to Vivian's discomfort. But she was quick to forgive me, and I, in turn, tried to be quick to snap out of it. We spent the whole afternoon going through Joan's trunk of family memorabilia, while Gordon and John watched a nice, manly game of Australian footie (football).

I confess I feel a bit guilty about describing my family discoveries when I should be writing only about cows and their place in the business world (omitting, of course, any reference to Don Quixote, whose place is among the venerable characters of literature). My colleagues at Dalhousie have no doubt cowed me into thinking I must always stick to the point. I have often wondered, however, why so many people seem to think that this is such a cardinal virtue. It must be true, or you wouldn't hear the phrase, "but I digress," ringing through the ages in such apologetic tones. It seems obvious to me that making connections on a broad basis is just as important as specializing in only one topic, but my friends from the groves of academe must have their reasons for thinking otherwise. But I digress…

It turned out to be a good thing that Gordon and I had been resting in Sydney for a week prior to the conference in Melbourne, for I think we were the only delegates there who didn't suffer from jet lag. As far as I could tell, we were the only ones who stayed awake during all the workshops and presentations. My favorite learning experiences, however, were associated with the "field trips" to various places where ordinary people were engaged in the practical work of getting on with life.

We had a most educational visit to a dairy farm where we watched 750 cows being milked on a carousel. The cows were funneled onto it through ever narrowing gates, which gave the animals no choice but to do what was expected of them. It took only two cowhands to get the job done – one to wipe the udders and attach the milking machine, and one to remove the machine and guide the cow off the carousel. The whole procedure took about five minutes per cow, but as the carousel held about 30 cows at a time, milking the herd took only two hours. Juergen Hagenow would have heartily approved of this system, which reduced labor by about 90%. Valerie and Vicki could have dispensed with the fly swatter once and for all.

One of my favorite field trips took us to a cattle breeding station where we were given a tour through the laboratories. A freckled, curly-headed genetic engineer gave us an informative and highly entertaining lecture about breeding methods, accompanied by slides. We all sat there in the semi-darkness, laughing ourselves silly over his running commentary. Two executives from Danone were sitting on my left, but I noticed they were unamused by the geneticist's humorous patter about the sex life of bovines.

It finally dawned on me, when I heard one of them ask the other in French what the lecture was all about, that neither of them spoke a word of English. I took pity on them and offered to translate the commentary for them. They turned out to be rather stuffy old fellows, or perhaps they considered themselves to be specimens of abnormally high breeding themselves, but I was unable to coax even the smallest, most delicate chortle from their tightly closed lips. They stared at me with expressions of inscrutable hauteur until the lecture was finally over. Then, without even a word of thanks, they slipped away into the crowd, leaving me completely baffled as to how two francophones who spoke no English expected to get anything out of a conference taking place in Australia. I never saw the two mysterious Frenchmen again, but I would have given anything to know what they had learned from the young geneticist's lively presentation.

For Gordon and me, however, the 23rd International Dairy Conference in Melbourne, my father's birthplace, was an unmitigated success. Our Australian hosts went all out to educate us, entertain us, and introduce us to the best their country had to offer, including its cuisine. We went away feeling impressed with our Aussie colleagues in the dairy industry, and we were delighted to have become acquainted with family members we had never met before.

Yogurt down the tubes

As we sat in the airplane heading back to Canada, Gordon and I had to admit that we had not come up with any bright new ideas to give our company the boost it needed to help it face the ever-growing competition from the multinationals, whose presence was becoming more and more apparent as we moved deeper into the '90s. The Europeans, it seemed, had all the advantages when it came to making yogurt. For one thing Europeans, and northern Europeans in particular, consumed ten times more yogurt per capita than Americans, and they exceeded Canadian per capita consumption by a factor of twenty.

We remembered a trip we had taken to the Netherlands back in the days when we were determined to find a way to mix fruit into our yogurt so as to disturb the product as little as possible and at the same time maintain the integrity of the big, juicy pieces of fruit. Our method, like everyone else's, was to pour the fruit into a vat of warm yogurt and then fold it in with an H-shaped baffle. By the time the fruit was thoroughly mixed into the product, however, the action of the baffle had broken the fruit into small pieces and had thinned down the yogurt to a consistency that failed to satisfy us. Our customers were not complaining, though, for everyone else's yogurt was just as thin, but we knew it could be thicker and more luscious if the baffle didn't play such havoc on it during the mixing process. Obviously some other technology was needed. It wasn't long before a Dutchman invented just such a process. Gordon read about it in his latest copy of *Dairy Foods* magazine, and he described it to me with enthusiasm.

"This guy is a genius," he said with quiet awe. "He's the only other person in the world who seems to care enough about yogurt to see the problem in the first place, but the amazing thing is that he also knew how to solve the problem, too! What he did was he took a large, stainless steel tube and mounted it on a 30 degree angle, then he attached a motor to it so it would slowly rotate while he gently poured yogurt and fruit into the upper end. The two products got gently folded into each other as they slowly slid down the rotating, tilted tube right into the hopper of a filling machine at the other end."

"I love it!" I said. "It's so simple and straightforward."

"That's the mark of genius," Gordon murmured, looking admiringly at a glossy photo of the tube. "I really want to see this thing in action. And if we like it as much as we think we will, maybe we can buy one from him."

We scooped up the girls, who were still in grade school at the time, and took them with us to the Netherlands. Their teachers were delighted that they'd be spending a week in Europe. They gave them some homework to do so they wouldn't be behind when they got back, and sent them off with their blessing.

The rotating tube turned out to be all we had hoped it would be, and the dairy manufacturer's demonstration run produced a yogurt to die for. But the tube turned out to be two storeys high, a detail that was not clearly brought out either in the article or by the photo in the magazine. Our yogurt plant was only a one-storey building, and there was no way in the world that the tube could be made to fit. A smaller tube would not allow enough product through, and a more acute angle would not permit the yogurt to travel at sufficient speed.

To alleviate our disappointment, our Dutch host took the time to show us through his dairy plant. He had nothing to fear, after all, from a Canadian manufacturer whose plant was not even big enough to accept the tube he had invented. This was a man who believed in making height work for him. His was a four-storey dairy plant, and his pasteurization vats were three-and-a-half storeys high. He had to take an elevator up to the fourth floor just to peek inside the vats. When we contemplated his stature, we could see how this kind of thinking might have taken hold. He stood fully 6' 7" tall in his bare feet. A typical Dutchman, in other words.

Gordon asked him how many stores he went to in the course of a week.

"I do about 350 stores, more or less," he replied, after a slight pause. "And they're all within an hour of the factory."

"Well, if your drivers had to travel for seven hours, as ours do, what would your market be then?"

"Oh, Paris, Rome, Moscow… The sky is the limit."

"And that," Gordon said sadly as we touched down in the Halifax airport, "is exactly why we're never going to be able to compete with the Europeans. Not only do they consume 20 times more yogurt than we do, but there are ten times more people in Europe than there are in Canada, and the whole place is not as big as Canada, either. So their dairy plants are huge, and when they decide to expand into our little province we won't stand a chance."

Gordon couldn't have foreseen that his prophecy would come true within a few short years.

A finger in the dike

Our search for new markets and new ideas had taken us all over the world, yet we still had not come up with a definite plan to put our company on firm ground. If we couldn't increase sales by penetrating new markets, was there some way we could improve the product itself? People who knew and loved our yogurt told us there was no possible way to improve it. They usually begged us, in fact, to leave it alone.

"Every time I see a product that claims to be *new and improved*," a friend of mine once said, "I know they've done something to make it cheaper and worse."

I recognized that my friend's comments were crucial to the continued success of our company. We definitely had a large group of loyal customers keeping us in business, but could they see us through the hard times that lay ahead? Our sales were slipping, due mainly to growing competition, and there seemed to be no way to change the tide. Well-meaning people would ask us why we didn't put on an advertising campaign, but they didn't realize how much it would cost to do it right. If there was one thing we had learned over the years, it was that if you don't have the money to mount a proper advertising campaign, then you're better off not advertising at all. It's just money down the drain.

We finally concluded that if we couldn't increase sales in a market that was growing more competitive every day, we could at least make an all-out effort to decrease costs. This was a painful process that made everyone irritable, but over time it eventually began to make a difference. We were surprised, in fact, to discover how many little careless money leakages there were in the company, and what a difference it made when we began in earnest to plug the holes in the dike. We turned off lights, we turned down heat, we put an end to personal phone calls (especially of the long distance variety), we requested the employees to pay for the yogurt and other ingredients they took home, and we eliminated every other unnecessary cost that we could think of, no matter how small. It was amazing how it all began to add up.

Then, just when we thought we were making some tangible progress in putting our little company back on track, the two supermarket chains took away half our shelf space to make room for the multinationals. And this takes us right back to where we were in Chapter One, where I started this saga *in medias res.*

Photo by George Thomas, Harrowsmith Magazine

Gordon poses with the eponymous Daisy.

Photo by Bob Brooks

Sonia and Gordon make yogurt in the kitchen.

*Gordon skims milk while Sonia stamps
expiry dates on yogurt containers.*

*Gordon mixes batter while Sonia checks
a recipe from her yogurt cookbook.*

We are the proud owners of a brand-new yogurt manufacturing plant.

Photo by George Thomas, Harrowsmith Magazine

Seven-year-old Valerie alights from the yogurt delivery truck. What a luxury it is to have a refrigerated box!

Ten years later we have a greatly expanded yogurt plant (left) with a loading dock, walk-in cooler, freezer, and incubator room. We also have several tractor-trailers and a farm house (right) that has become the administrative headquarters for Peninsula Farm. The boat in the background is unfortunately not ours.

Two of the six tractor-trailers are in the loading dock waiting to be readied for the next week's deliveries.

Let there be light.

And now there is... a light version of Peninsula Farm's excellent yogourt. To make something better it's not only what you add, but what you're left with. Peninsula Farm's new Light Yogourt has only 1% milk fat. That's 60% less than the traditional recipe. But it still has the same great taste. And the same natural goodness in every container. Fresh milk. Fresh frozen berries. No preservatives. No artificial flavour or colour.

Peninsula Farm Light Yogourt is in your grocery store now with a choice of 6

delicious offerings including **Cherry, Lemon, Coffee, Strawberry Banana, Plain Skimmed Milk, and new Berry Best**... an appetizing blend of raspberries, blueberries and strawberries. **To shed a little more light on the subject, read Sonia Jones'**

new book *It all began with Daisy*, the story of Peninsula Farm — a story of hard work, nutritious eating and a healthy respect for the people who love the world's finest yogourt — Peninsula Farm.

Distributed by Podberry and Whitestair. Ask for it at your local bookseller.

Design by Greg Silver

Our newest product now is a line-up of low-fat yogurt for the health-conscious generation. We still maintained our full-fat yogurt at that point, but we were glad to have extra cream for the ice-cream and the sour cream which were becoming more and more popular.

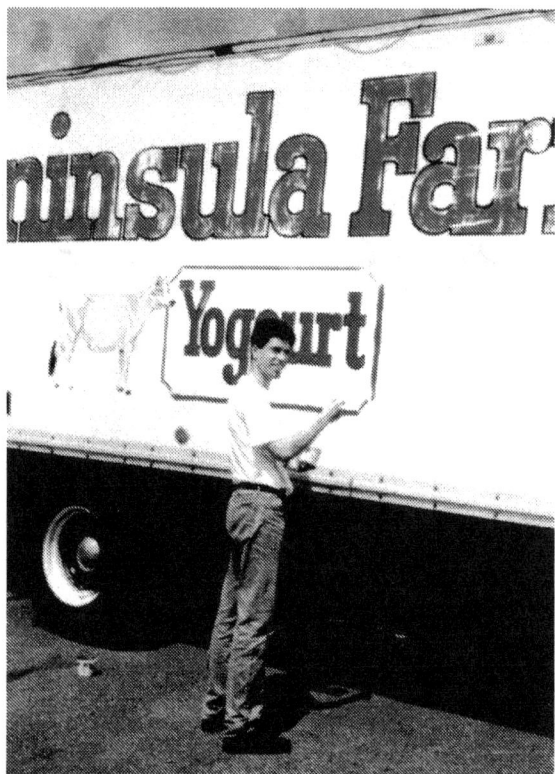

Simon Bovenga repaints a trailer.

Gordon discusses a problem with programmer David Bruce.

Gordon talks to customers about Peninsula Farm yogurt, while grandson Harrison checks out the product on the bottom shelf.

Gordon and Sonia stand by the filling machine in the yogurt plant.

A large sign on First Peninsula points people to the oceanside farm.

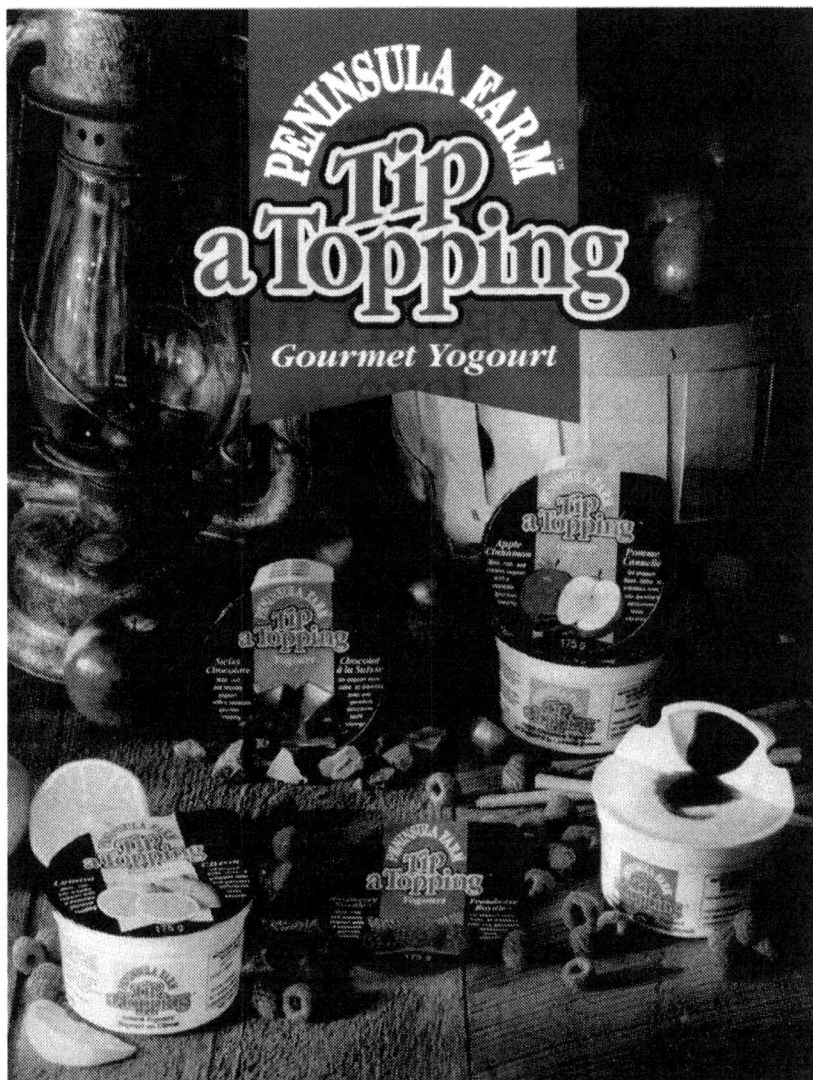

PENINSULA FARM
Tip a Topping
Gourmet Yogourt

After discovering this dual container in Germany, we became the first to introduce the concept to the Canadian market. We called our new product "Tip a Topping" because the plain yogurt was on one side and the fruit topping was on the other. After peeling off the foil lid, the customer could tip the topping over the yogurt by bending the plastic hinge in the middle, thus creating a sundae-style treat. Our line-up included raspberry, strawberry, blueberry, lemon, cinnamon apple, and chocolate.

Plant Manager Bill Towndrow double checks the yogurt in one of the trailers before driver Jimmy Pittman takes it on the road.

Distribution manager Blair Landry checks his calculations before letting Bill Towndrow know how much yogurt will be needed for the following week's production.

Sonia at a book-signing for "It All Began With Daisy," published by Penguin/EP Dutton in New York.

Cheryl Lohnes (Accounts Receivable) took this photo of her kitten, Fuddly (Dudley's sister).

We welcome "Good Morning, America" (ABC/TV) with a decorated Peninsula Farm cheesecake.

After the federal inspectors got through with their vandalization project we erected a monument to Daisy, without whom life would not have been nearly as challenging or interesting. A beautiful brown cow in the green, green grass, she stands on a pedestal in the meadow behind the farm house, gazing out to sea. The bush in front of her comes alive with flowers every spring, bringing to mind the cycle of life and the hope extended to all creatures great and small.

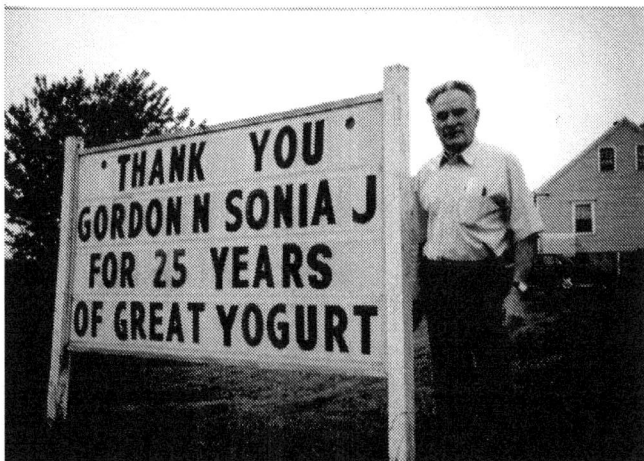

Gordon stands by a sign posted on Elvin Falkenham's farm in Lunenburg. It was a comfort to know that people supported us so whole-heartedly.

This illustration by Pete Bentovoja appeared in the Los Angeles Times to accompany the article written by Sonia Jones.

Valerie and her husband, Steven Zlotkus,
on their wedding day.

Victoria is married to Kenton Grassmid in
Puerto Vallarta, Mexico.

CHAPTER TWELVE

Desperate Counter-measures

The handwriting on the wall

Drastic changes require desperate counter-measures. There was no reasoning with anyone at either of the two supermarket chains, not even with David Sobey himself. He was semi-retired now, so he passed me back to the very men who had made the decision to cut my shelf space in the first place. The arguments were the same in both chain stores: *Your sales are slipping, so we've reduced your space.* My answer was also the same as well: *My sales have not gone down by half. But they will, now that you've taken away half my shelf space. Please reconsider.*

But they refused. The truth of the matter was that they were getting more profit from the multinationals, and there was nothing I could do about that. Where do you draw the line? They were getting a fair profit from me, and they always had. But they were getting a greater profit from the food giants, and they liked that better.

"It's not just greed, Mrs. Jones, if that's what you're thinking," said one of the head buyers. "You know yourself what it's like to have to struggle to stay profitable. Well, it's the same for us, only on a larger scale. We always have to keep an eye on the bottom line. If we don't, then the boys across the street will get ahead of us, and if they do, we're in big trouble. All they need is a tiny edge, then it gets worse and worse till they win the war. We have our problems too. You're not the only one who's fighting to stay alive."

I understood what he was telling me, but I didn't like it, and I didn't see where I could fit into the picture. From what he was saying I had to deduce that the whole world would eventually be owned by a handful of companies. Make that one enormous company. Why not? Conglomerates were already going in that direction. So where did that leave small businesses? Where did that leave small countries, for that matter?

The most discouraging thing about it was that it really didn't matter any more how good you were. It didn't matter if you invented the best mouse trap in the world, you would be swallowed up anyway. How do you stop a tidal wave? And what was to become of our company motto: *If you have to be the smallest, then you'd better be the best*?

It seemed to me that the only hope lay in the community itself. There were many people in Nova Scotia who could read the handwriting on the wall. There were also people, therefore, who could read the handwriting on the labels, too, and were very happy to buy products made by small, local companies. In return they got value for their money. They were buying fresh food from farmers' markets, and they were getting pure, fresh yogurt mixed with real fruit from small companies like ours. They were supporting their communities, and we needed to do everything we could to show them that this was a viable alternative to globalization. Together we had the power to turn the tide. Together we might even have the power to stop a tidal wave.

If there was nothing I could do to persuade the chains not to cut my shelf space (and therefore my sales) in half, then I would have to take the desperate counter-measure of cutting my costs (and therefore my company) in half. Gordon and I stayed up night after night, working out how this could be done. We would have to discontinue delivering yogurt to those regions in the Maritime Provinces that were either unprofitable because they were unpopulated, or unprofitable because they were too far away. This meant Cape Breton and Yarmouth, the two opposite ends of Nova Scotia, and northern New Brunswick.

After consulting carefully with Blair, we concluded that once we made the necessary changes to the delivery routes, we'd be able to sell three of our five tractor-trailers, keeping the straight truck for Halifax. This meant we'd have to lay off three truck drivers and all the merchandisers responsible for the stores on the canceled routes. That was the hard part. The drivers and merchandisers had been with us for many years. It was like losing family.

"We may have some trouble implementing this plan," I said to Gordon. "The head offices of both chains told me some time ago that I couldn't just pick and choose the stores I wanted. It wouldn't be fair to the outlying communities, they said. Every product has to be available to every customer in every region. That's their policy."

I went back to the chain store buyers and explained to them what our plan was, and how we could not survive unless we cut out all the unprofitable stores. They frowned, but both chains accepted our decision. After doing us such immense harm, they could afford to be kind in smaller ways

We'd have to move fast. Once the sales went down, our response had to be immediate or the hemorrhage would do us in. Three of the six plant workers had to be let go. One of the three office workers would have to be laid off as well.

Sylvia volunteered. She had been planning for some time to start an accounting business of her own, and now that she had finished upgrading her qualifications, she felt the time was right to move on.

As it turned out, Peninsula Farm became her very first customer. Her knowledge of the company was too valuable for us to let it go up in smoke, so the arrangement benefited both parties. This left one of the other office workers with some free time, so Crystal, who had started out working in the plant years ago, resumed her work there whenever she was needed.

On the fourth day of crisis management Blair came to us and said he wanted to take us to lunch.

"Blair, you can't leave too," I said, sensing what he was going to say. "What would we do without you?"

He looked down at his feet. He told us he would never think of leaving us if he didn't believe it was necessary. But he'd given it a lot of thought, and he didn't see how we could afford to keep him any longer.

"There isn't anything I can do that you guys can't do too," he said. "After all, you taught me everything I know."

"There are only so many hours in the day," Gordon said.

"I know, I've thought about that. But Craig could be the plant manager. And he's good with money, too. He can pinch a nickel so hard he can make the beaver fart."

We had to laugh at that one, but we had tears in our eyes.

"Who'll be in charge of merchandising?" I asked. Blair had always done Nova Scotia on the days when he wasn't really needed on the plant floor.

"Well, we've got Janet in New Brunswick," he said, "and I know Norman would love to be the merchandising manager for Nova Scotia. He'd need a raise, but he's definitely your best bet. He's been with us for years, and he's as fast as lightning."

I knew from his quick answers that Blair had been giving everything a lot of thought before he came to chat with us, so it was hopeless to try to get him to change his mind about leaving. That didn't stop me from trying anyway.

"I've already got another job," he confessed finally, when I pressed him further.

He had accepted a position as General Manager of the Halifax branch of a large trucking company, and he would be starting at a higher salary than we could afford to pay him.

"It's not the money," he said, looking at us with pleading eyes. "You know I'd rather work for you. But I do have a wife and two kids now, and I have to think of them too."

I knew he meant what he said about liking his job with us. He was his own boss, he called the shots when and how he saw fit, he made his own hours, and he was completely free to come and go as he pleased. He had all the advantages of a business owner, without any of the risks and responsibilities. I had to smile when I recalled the many times he had nobly declared that he was taking full responsibility for whatever it was that had gone wrong. He had the best intentions, I'm sure, in claiming responsibility that way, and I'm equally sure he won points with his plant workers for deflecting the blame away from them. But when the time came to pay the bills for all the honest mistakes and careless errors, I often caught myself wondering just what it meant to "take responsibility" for a problem when somebody else has to pay for it.

Ah well, life goes on. Blair would soon be wearing a shirt and tie and showing up for work promptly at nine o'clock. He would have to study reams of operations manuals and deal with fifty or sixty truck drivers on a daily basis. He would find out what it was like to work for a multinational corporation. But the pay was good and the job was reasonably secure, so who could blame him? It was everybody's dream, that kind of a job. The transport company was lucky to have an intelligent, hard-working man like Blair, too. But I couldn't help thinking, when we said goodbye to our young protégé, that we were probably not the only small company to lose our top executive to a multinational corporation. Goliath was here to stay.

The bells continued to toll.

Too late to sell out

Gordon and I stared blankly at the empty desks in the offices of our former farm house. There was a sense of sorrow and defeat about it all, but we knew we would have to pull ourselves up by the boot straps as quickly as possible to instill some sense of morale in the remaining employees. We sat down at the conference table to write a few notes about the possible upside of the latest disaster, but we began reminiscing instead about the many opportunities we had once had to sell the company at various times in the past.

We experienced the first nibbles back in the '80s when we had been approached by one of our local competitors. They couldn't make us any kind of a purchase offer, not even based on a ballpark figure, until they'd seen our sales figures for the previous three years. Then they needed to see the distribution figures by store and territory, they explained, or it would be impossible for them to calculate their costs. Then, after we had dutifully provided them with all the information they were looking for, they told us they weren't interested after all.

When I asked them why, they said it would be unfair to the Quebec dairy whose yogurt they already distributed. When I asked them why they didn't think of that in the first place, they attempted to flatter me into believing they would much rather make their own yogurt than distribute somebody else's, and they would have been proud to make and own the Peninsula Farm brand. But that would mean becoming enemies with the Quebec manufacturer who, after all, was a direct competitor.

I felt like asking them why it didn't bother them to become enemies with us, but by that time I knew I had been suckered out of my sales information by a competitor that had never seriously wanted to buy my company in the first place. My suspicions were soon proven right when the would-be Nova Scotia buyers put the Quebec yogurt that they distributed on a deep-discount special in all the stores where our sales were highest. I can't bear to even think about how stupid I had been to reveal my sales figures to a competitor.

Then a couple of years later, along came a second local competitor who tried to do the same thing. But once bitten, twice shy. When I told him I was unwilling to share my private information with him, he quickly trotted out a "confidentiality agreement" which legally obligated him to keep any information I gave him completely confidential. He assured me he'd never reveal anything to my competitors. Any information I gave him would go no further.

Well of course not! My competitors were his competitors too, so why would he want to help them by giving them my sales figures? What's more, of what use is a confidentiality agreement if he himself is the very person to whom I wouldn't want to reveal my sales information?

I was hesitant to tell him, though, that his confidentiality agreement was pointless. It could embarrass him if I let him know that I knew he was trying to play me for a fool, and I also knew that an embarrassed competitor might want to seek revenge. Not that it really mattered in the long run. There's an old Spanish proverb that says that whether the (iron) pot hits the (clay) pitcher or the pitcher hits the pot, it's going to be bad for the pitcher. When it came to my competitors, Peninsula Farm pretty much always got the brunt of it.

"If you give me some sort of payment to prove to me that you're really interested," I said finally, "then I'll show you the figures. The more you pay, the more details you get."

"No, no, no, it just doesn't work that way I'm afraid," he laughed, acting as though I were the one who was trying to get the best of *him*. "I'm not laying out any cash till I know what I'm paying for. You'll have to make me a full disclosure, or we have nothing more to discuss."

And that was the end of that. I was puzzled that the local dairies, who had the most to gain by slipping me into their already existing infrastructure, were the very ones who for some reason were never willing to buy us out. Peninsula Farm was much less valuable to companies outside the Maritimes, where our name was relatively unknown. Our physical plant was also of little interest, since it was too small to be of much use to anybody but us. It looked as though Gordon and I would just have to keep plugging away forever.

The upside of downsizing

It turned out, however, that being forced to chop our company in half was not the disaster (financially) that we thought it would be. Cutting out the fat is probably something that all sensible companies need to do every once in a while, but a small family business generally has a particularly difficult time facing this necessary evil. Laying off employees who have become what amounts to family members is a heart-wrenching affair. And disappointing loyal customers in outlying regions is also an extremely difficult thing to have to do. But we were impressed with the efficiencies that resulted from a reduced staff, and we were moved by the fact that a good number of customers seemed to be coming in from outlying areas to buy our yogurt in the larger cities.

After watching our books very carefully for the next four weeks, I got together with Sylvia to do a cost/benefit analysis of our obligatory downsizing. We discovered that although the downside was not as deadly as we thought it would be, it did not have quite the upside we expected, either. There was only one thing left to do. It was what we feared and disliked more than anything else: we would have to raise our prices.

It was no use raising them just a little bit. Doing it by increments would have been an irritation both to the customers and to the chains as well, so we decided to go all the way and raise the prices to a level that would provide us with a small profit. Not only is it discouraging to work for nothing, but it is downright dangerous. Banks and creditors expect to be paid, after all, and we had always enjoyed a clean record with them. We wanted to keep it that way. So up went the prices along with our heartbeats.

To our profound astonishment and eternal gratitude, the sales held at the previous levels. Our customers were talking to us with their pocketbooks, and we could have hugged each and every one of them. We breathed an incredibly grateful and affectionate sigh of relief, and continued working with renewed hope and energy. It looked as though our little company might actually be here to stay.

CHAPTER THIRTEEN

Just When we Thought it was Safe...

The axe falls

There comes a time in life when critical, sometimes devastating changes take place, often when we least expect them. A woman in rural Quebec will give birth to quintuplets, a resident of a small town will win ten million dollars in the national lottery, or a con artist will wipe out the life savings of a kind-hearted old pensioner. We tend to lay it down to an act of God, or to especially good or bad luck. But seldom do we imagine that ordinary individuals with painfully commonplace jobs can create such sudden and life-changing effects.

Yet that's how it happened to Gordon and me. At 9:00 am on Tuesday, June 4th, 2002, a black, nondescript car pulled into our yard, took a slow turn around the asphalt circle, and came to a halt next to the retaining wall by the loading dock. A moment later there was a sharp knock on our factory door.

We knew an official from the Canadian Food Inspection Agency was coming to take a look at the plant. But what we didn't anticipate, and what affected us all in such a drastic way, was the outcome of the inspection.

Gordon was in the middle of loading cases of yogurt onto a pallet when he heard the knocking. Michelle, who was standing at the end of the filling machine packing cardboard cases with yogurt coming off the belt, looked apprehensively at the door.

"Do I have to answer that right away?" she asked Gordon.

"We can't stop the filling machine," he said.

Michelle already knew the answer, but she wanted Gordon to make the decision. Kirk, who was measuring fruit and mixing it into a batch of yogurt, had not even heard the knocking. Craig was too busy replenishing the lid and cup dispensers to pay any attention to the disturbance.

The knocking grew louder.

Gordon frowned. The cost of stopping the filling machine was simply too great, and no one else was available to go to the door. It annoyed him, too, that he was going to have to take the time to explain everything to a new inspector who had never visited the plant before. Production was sure to be held up by several hours that day while he and Craig showed him the operation. He was bound to have questions about how the machinery worked in a factory that was, by all accounts, one of the smallest dairy plants in Canada.

It was quite an accomplishment that Gordon and the staff, both past and present, had managed to figure out how to produce yogurt in such relatively small quantities. The whole factory was a minor miracle of creative design coupled with the innovative use of stainless steel equipment, some of which was more likely to be found in industrial kitchens than in a dairy plant. But their efforts had paid off, and Gordon was proud of all his employees for their contribution to "the little plant that could." He hoped the inspector would be duly impressed, but he wasn't going to hold his breath.

The knocking became more insistent.

Gordon didn't want to get off on the wrong foot with this individual, for it was the first time that the federal government had become involved in the inspection of our dairy plant. For the past 25 years provincial inspectors had been responsible for overseeing our operation, but the federal government had come up with the idea that it should be their responsibility to inspect any food plant shipping products over provincial borders. That included us, because for the past twenty years we'd been sending yogurt to our neighboring provinces, New Brunswick and Prince Edward Island.

But why now? Why were the federal inspectors taking over the duties of the provincial inspectors? We were at a loss to explain it to ourselves or to our employees. We had worked well with the provincial inspectors, and we didn't see how things could improve now that the federal inspectors had become involved, but we were not privy to the inner workings of our government. Perhaps there was a tug-of-war going on between the federal and provincial inspectors over territorial issues. Or maybe the public had become nervous because of the scandal in Walkerton, a town in Ontario where the drinking water was contaminated. Perhaps it was just a case of empire-building on the part of some ambitious civil servants who wanted their little portion of the government to be larger and more important. Or maybe certain individuals were looking for job security by drumming up some extra work to justify their salaries. It was hard to say. All we knew was that Canada had the reputation of being a very top-heavy country where government employment was concerned.

There was a sharp rapping at the door once again.

"You want me to turn off the filling machine?" Michelle shouted, above the clanking of the mechanical parts.

"No," Gordon said. "We're almost done. If you turn it off in the middle of everything, there'll be a mess to clean up. Then the inspector will scribble it all down on his notepad and he'll complain about yogurt being on the plant floor."

When Gordon was finally able to open the door, he was astonished to see not one federal inspector, but four of them gathered at the threshold, looking dour and officious. One of the men introduced himself as Bill Bishop. He strode past Gordon and approached the filling machine with the other three inspectors in tow. The four of them spent the rest of the day asking questions and taking interminable notes.

"Can you imagine?" said Gordon at the dinner table that night. "The feds sent four inspectors to our plant. *Four!* One for each of us. Doesn't that seem like overkill to you? The whole thing was even worse than I imagined. I had to take time off to explain everything right down to the last detail."

"Did they know anything, or did you have to tell them?"

"Hard to say. They do the asking, they don't do the talking. They try not to reveal anything about themselves. But I had the impression right from the start that they had a hidden agenda. They weren't like the provincial inspectors. I had the feeling they weren't interested in helping us or working with us, either. They just stood there asking questions and taking notes. I felt as though I couldn't get through to them, no matter what I said. It was weird. I really had this strong feeling that they wanted to do me some kind of harm."

"Do you really think they were out to get you?"

"That's what it seemed like to me. And you know I'm not paranoid. I get along with most people, but there was no talking to those guys. Actually, they weren't all guys. There was a woman there, too. They all seemed to look to her for direction. She was smarter than the rest of them and I'm sure they knew it. They'd never want to admit it, of course."

"Well, when are they going to give us the verdict?"

"Tomorrow. They all booked themselves into a bed-and-breakfast down by the waterfront, and they're going to write up a report for us to see in the morning."

"Does it take four people to write a report? That's a pretty heavy burden for the taxpayers, isn't it?"

"You got it. Four square meals. Four rooms at the inn. A nice little walk along the boardwalk after dinner. Pretty good life, wouldn't you say?"

"You said it. It's always easy for the critics. The hard part is for the people who get the ideas, put up the money, and do the actual work."

Impossible tests

The next day, Wednesday, June 5th, Bill Bishop and the other inspectors returned to Peninsula Farm and met with Gordon and our plant manager, who had just finished the day's yogurt production. The inspectors sat themselves comfortably around our dining room table and announced that as a result of their observations they had come to the conclusion that Peninsula Farm's ability to successfully pasteurize milk was in doubt.

"What?" said Gordon, unable to believe his ears. "What on earth makes you think *that?*"

"We're not here to explain anything now, Mr. Jones," said Bishop. "We're simply delivering our observations."

"Just hold on a minute," Gordon said, his face reddening. "I think I have the right to know why you're saying we don't know how to pasteurize milk properly. We've been doing it for twenty-five years!"

"It will all be written up in our report."

"But pasteurizing milk is what we do best!" Gordon said. "You can't possibly claim that we're doing it wrong!"

The four inspectors sat back and patiently allowed Gordon to explain to them that it was our policy to pasteurize the milk at 85°C, a much higher temperature than what is required by the dairy regulations, which stipulate that the milk be pasteurized at 68°C. He also explained that we hold the milk at 85°C for half an hour, whereas the dairy regulations only call for it to be held for 10 seconds at 68°C. It was obvious that we greatly exceeded the dairy regulations in our pasteurization process.

"We've learned that the higher temperature and longer holding time 'cleans' the milk better than if we just took it to the pasteurization temperature you require," Gordon told them. "So what makes you think that we're not pasteurizing our milk successfully?"

"How do we know that you're actually doing what you say you're doing?" Bishop countered.

Gordon stared at him in disbelief.

"Didn't you hear what I just said? You can't make good yogurt if you don't pasteurize the milk, and you can't make excellent yogurt if you don't de-activate the enzymes by heat-treating the milk, and to do that you have to take it way beyond the point of mere pasteurization."

"What, exactly, are your procedures?" the woman asked.

Gordon fought hard to be patient. "I personally check the temperatures indicated by the thermometers in the vats, and I do this throughout the pasteurization and cooling process. I also manually annotate these temperatures in my records."

"Your personal records don't prove a thing," Bishop said. "We need records produced mechanically and recorded on paper, so we can keep the records on file."

"Oh, so *that's* what you're worried about," said Gordon, looking relieved. "Well, that's no problem at all. We have a beautiful computer logging program that was devised by an expert we hired especially to do the job. It works perfectly."

"Where are the written records for today's production?"

"The printer is being fixed just now, but I can have them for you tomorrow. I can give you records that go back as far as you like, but you'll have to wait till tomorrow morning. Meanwhile I can show you anything you want to see on the computer monitor. It's all there on the hard drive."

"Well, if you don't have written records we have no proof that you are pasteurizing your milk successfully," Bishop said, with a hint of satisfaction.

"I just told you, I can show you the *monitor*! It's all right there on the screen. It's just not on paper, that's all. But I can get the written records to you tomorrow. You'll love it. Our computer generates a chart recording of all the temperatures throughout the pasteurization and cooling process. And it's recorded in a different color ink for every vat in the plant."

But the inspectors stubbornly continued to nurture their inexplicable doubts. They pointed out that they had no proof that our indicating thermometer was accurate or that our computer was properly calibrated with the thermometer.

"All you have to do is look at the computer screen and look at the thermometer, and you'll see with your own eyes that the reading is exactly the same!"

But no, the inspectors clearly didn't trust their own eyes. Instead, they ordered Gordon to bring in a technician to check the calibration of the thermometer and our computer recording system. The inspectors all agreed that technicians from Darose Control Systems Limited would be the obvious choice.

As the meeting adjourned, Bishop gave Gordon a letter stating that certain conditions had to be met before product made at our plant could be shipped interprovincially. We were asked to provide the CFIA with documentation proving that pasteurization had occurred on each batch of product, and proof of pasteurization was to be provided by an acceptable lab analysis completed by a laboratory approved by the CFIA.

When I saw the letter later that day I was hard-pressed to understand how a lab test on the finished product could prove that our milk had been pasteurized. Such a test would only prove that the finished product was free of whatever pathogens were sought by the methods applied, but the absence of pathogens could not in themselves *prove* that the milk had been pasteurized, since the milk could have been pathogen-free before the pasteurization process took place.

The presence of pathogens, on the other hand, could raise doubts about the pasteurization process, but even then there'd be no proof that unsuccessful pasteurization was at fault, since pathogens could enter the product by other pathways after the milk had been pasteurized. The CFIA inspectors were barking up the wrong tree. It was much more plausible to me that our computer chart recording system, once it was examined and approved by the technicians from Darose Control, would provide the only incontrovertible proof that the milk had indeed been pasteurized successfully.

"There's simply no way any lab can provide them with proof that the yogurt was made with pasteurized milk," I told Gordon. "They'll just have to be satisfied with the findings of Darose Control. And I know they'll find everything in order."

"I hope you're right," Gordon said. "But I still have the feeling they're trying to find something to complain about."

"You don't think they were... you don't think they've been influenced by some competitor, do you?"

"I'd never want to even suggest such a thing unless I had solid proof. And I don't see how we'd ever get it, either. I don't know. I just don't like the direction this thing is taking."

"Well, we know we have nothing to worry about. Our fresh yogurt has always passed inspection. And it's never been recalled. So it'll all turn out all right in the end."

"I don't know," Gordon said dubiously. "We still haven't seen the end of it. Take a look at this."

He handed me the "action plan" that had to be filled out before any yogurt could be distributed interprovincially. We were being asked to explain how we intended to address each item mentioned in their report.

"This is going to cost us a fortune," I groaned, looking at the many pages that Gordon had placed in my hand. "But at least they're giving us plenty of time to make the changes, which proves they're not all that urgent. It'll be expensive, but it won't put us out of business."

"You hope," said Gordon, sighing heavily.

"Well, it all boils down to three things," I said. "I'll fill out the action plan, and I'll make sure the yogurt tests get done just as soon as they tell me what they want. Meanwhile you can call Darose Control, and ask them to come over right away. Tell them it's urgent, okay? Oh, and ask Craig to run you off some hard copy of the computer records. The rest we can do little by little. It's a nuisance, but we can do it."

"Who knows how much time we'll have to waste before they're satisfied?" Gordon said, looking dejected. "The problem is, it's hard for me to imagine them ever being satisfied with anything, no matter what we do."

In violation of the law

On Thursday, June 6th, after completing the day's production, we received a letter from the Food Safety Specialist with the CFIA, stating that because the inspectors had doubts about our ability to pasteurize our milk successfully, we were in violation of Sections 4 and 7 of the Food and Drugs Act. We were astonished to be told that we were violating the law when the inspectors had no proof that there was anything wrong with our pasteurization methods or with the yogurt itself.

We still had no idea what their "doubts" were based on. Moreover, if the inspectors were really so concerned about our pasteurization process one would think they would have immediately recalled the yogurt from the stores. This action was not taken, presumably because our pasteurization methods of the previous week (the same we had used for over 20 years) had resulted in a product that had been tested every week and had been found to be perfectly safe and normal.

When Gordon questioned the inspectors further, he was told that there had been no complaints about our yogurt. What's more, they gave no indication that their doubts about the safety of our product were based on anything tangible, such as, for example, a test that could have been performed on samples of our yogurt taken from stores prior to the inspection day. It seemed incredible to us that after 26 years of producing fresh yogurt that had never been recalled from the stores, it should suddenly occur to the CFIA that at this particular moment it was necessary for them to doubt our ability to pasteurize milk.

If we were puzzled by the groundless doubts expressed by the inspectors and surprised to learn that we were therefore in violation of the Food and Drugs Act, we were also greatly concerned by the third paragraph of the memo we received that day. The inspectors, in their wisdom, had decided to impound our yogurt. The memo informed us that the products in our refrigerated warehouse could not be sold until a peroxidase test was performed to determine whether or not the pasteurization process had been completed successfully. I noted that the word "interprovincially" was now missing from the directive, but I hoped it was an oversight. I decided to let it rest for the time being and tackle the issues one at a time, starting with the mysterious peroxidase test.

I had never heard of this test, and the reason was simple. When I asked a microbiology lab to perform this procedure, I was informed by a technician that such a test could not be done on yogurt, as it was designed to detect only the *presence* of bacteria in a food product. Since yogurt teems with (beneficial) bacteria, the peroxidase test, which was designed to test items such as frozen food, would necessarily yield a false positive.

I called Mike Fullerton, the inspector who had apparently been appointed by Bishop to represent the group, and told him that the test could not be done and why. He said he'd consult with his colleagues to see if they could come up with something else. Meanwhile he instructed me to get the "action plan" to him as quickly as possible, as it was one of the three prerequisites for releasing the yogurt that had been impounded (the other two being the peroxidase test and the investigation to be carried out by the technicians at Darose Control).

I stayed up most of the night to complete the action plan, which I faxed to the inspectors the next morning, along with a computer-generated chart of the times and temperatures of the milk heating process which Craig had produced from the newly-repaired printer that had been delivered early that day.

Later that morning I received a call from Mike Fullerton informing me that he and his colleagues had done some research and had come up with the idea that we should submit the impounded yogurt to an alkaline phosphatase test, since the peroxidase test was not suitable for testing yogurt.

Gordon and I quickly packed a cooler with yogurt samples and set off for a microbiology lab in the hopes that this test could be performed successfully. We called the lab on the car phone and outlined our plan, whereupon we were told that this test could not be done on yogurt either, as it, too, tested merely for the *presence* of bacteria and would also provide a false positive. There was nothing for it but to turn around and drive home again. We stored the yogurt in our refrigerator in case it was needed at some future time.

After informing Fullerton that the second test he requested could not be done on our product either, he confessed that he would have to consult the internet to see if he could find a suitable methodology for testing yogurt.

"There was no reason for them to come here to do a plant inspection, anyway," Gordon sputtered. "All they had to do was check the records of the provincial inspectors who have already tested the yogurt that's on the store shelves right now. I have their reports and they state that there are no pathogens, period. So that should have been the end of it. The government could save millions by firing all but a skeleton crew of inspectors and just doing product lab tests. If the products are clean in the lab, there's obviously no need for inspections. It's all a farce, that's what it is."

Outdated regulations

The following day two technicians from Darose Control Systems showed up at our plant to perform their tests on our equipment. They stated that the indicating thermometer was accurate and reading the proper temperature. The recording data logger read correctly on one channel and the other two channels read 0.5°C higher than the indicating thermometer, which fell well within accepted tolerances.

We were delighted to learn about the excellent results of the technicians' investigation. I called Fullerton to tell him the good news and to ask him to please release the impounded yogurt. He said he would need a written report from Darose Control Systems, so I called the technicians on their car phone and asked them to fax their report to the CFIA as soon as they got back to their office. I checked with Mike Fullerton a little later to see if he had received the report. He had.

"So could you please release our yogurt now?" I asked him, trying to control my impatience.

"I'm sorry, Mrs. Jones, but we can't do that just now."

"But why not?"

"Our regulations don't have any sort of description of your particular method of charting your pasteurization temperatures with a computer."

"Of course not. We developed the method ourselves."

"Perhaps that explains why it's not in our regulations."

"Well, naturally. But the provincial inspectors accepted our computer charting method, and they were pleased we had come up with such an accurate and innovative approach. They even said they thought that other dairies would want to adopt our state-of-the-art method in years to come!"

"I'm not going to comment on the decisions made by the provincial inspectors. My job is to implement the regulations of the federal government, and your system is not mentioned anywhere in our regulations. So it's unacceptable, I'm afraid."

"Then why did you make us send for the technicians from Darose Control? Why did you say they should check our equipment for accuracy? Why did you make us pay them to do something that you already knew would be unacceptable to you because it's not mentioned in your regulations?"

"The point is, Mrs. Jones, you must be compliant with the regulations of the federal government," said Fullerton, refusing to provide a clear answer to my direct questions. "And it's my job to see that you are."

"I still don't understand what the problem is."

"The problem, Mrs. Jones, is that your procedures do not comply with our regulations," said Fullerton, with the sort of forced patience that suggests a certain degree of intellectual deficiency on the part of the listener. "Therefore, we've decided that you'll have to replace your computer charting system with the vat-mounted chart recorders described in our regulations."

"Then why are you surfing the net looking for tests to do on our yogurt? What difference will it make, anyway? I don't understand!"

"We're going to test the yogurt that we're holding in your cooling room so we can find out if you're able to pasteurize milk successfully," he said, speaking slowly in an effort to help me grasp the situation clearly.

"And if you find out that we are, in fact, pasteurizing our milk correctly, will you let us keep our computer system? And will you release our yogurt then?" I felt a bit like Moses asking Pharaoh to let his people go.

"If the tests prove that you are pasteurizing your milk successfully," said Pharaoh, "you can sell the impounded yogurt. But you'll still have to replace your computer recording system with vat-mounted chart recorders, in compliance with federal regulations."

I tried to explain to him (very slowly and clearly so that he could understand) that this unnecessary procedure would be costly and lead to serious delays, especially when added to the work stoppage already caused by the perceived necessity of finding a test for the impounded yogurt, but my objections fell on deaf ears. Unfortunately I was not in a position to threaten him with twelve deadly plagues.

We try to pick up the pieces

When Gordon called David Rose at Darose Control to find out what it would cost to install the vat-mounted chart recorders that the federal inspectors demanded, he was told it would come to about $18,000 for materials and labor alone, not to mention unforeseen costs of one kind or another.

"Can you imagine scrapping a perfectly good computer monitoring system and replacing it with a retrograde method like vat-mounted chart recorders?" said Gordon, beside himself. "It would be like the army saying that all soldiers had to use rifles from now on and that the missiles and rocket launchers had to be scrapped because they're not described in the guidelines that were held over from the last war."

"They're giving us the run-around all right," I said. "First they wanted us to test the yogurt we made this week with tests that can't be done, and now we're supposed to get rid of the computer. It's absurd."

"And that's not all," Gordon said. "I haven't told you the worst part yet. David Rose called and said that delivery and installation of the vat-mounted chart recorders would take about ten weeks."

"Ten weeks!" I cried. "You talked about unforeseen costs for material and labor, but think about unforeseen time lost while we're waiting for the delivery and while they send us the wrong equipment, and while we wait for the guys to come and do the work!"

"Exactly. Remember how it was when we were building the factory? They sent us the wrong grout for the tile floor, then they sent us the right grout but not enough of it, then they told us the right grout wasn't being made any more, then we had to order the wrong grout again and mix it with the right grout, and that was just the beginning of all our troubles and costs and delays. You can count on it, whether you're building a factory or a house or installing equipment, you're going to have to pay double and wait twice as long as the estimate says."

"And remember that contractor?" I said. "He blamed the manufacturers, and customs officials, and truckers, and shippers and receivers, and clerical errors. He never had the equipment he needed because nobody could send it to him. And he never showed up to work on the factory when he said he would, because he spread himself so thin between all his other jobs. He acted as though the delays had nothing to do with him, when in fact nobody else was telling him what to do or how much work to take on. And you couldn't fire him, because he'd already started the work, and had received our down payment to boot."

"You can bet your bottom dollar that the inspectors know nothing about all these built-in costs and delays that everybody else knows about if they've ever run a business," said Gordon. "Come to think of it, it was the inspectors themselves who were actually behind all the grout problems because they were the ones who demanded that we have a tile floor in the first place. If they hadn't insisted on that tile floor, we wouldn't have needed the grout in the first place. And to top it all off, they changed their minds later, or they changed their regulations, or whatever, and then they said we shouldn't have a tile floor, we should put in a cement floor, so we had to lay cement on top of those expensive, unnecessary tiles!"

"They don't care," I said. "That's *our* problem, as far as they're concerned."

"And yet, and yet… they're almost going out of their way to make things impossible for us. What's the point?"

"That's exactly it. We keep going around in circles. We could drive ourselves crazy."

"Yes, and they could drive us out of business, and that's worse," said Gordon. "They'll deep six the whole company, then they'll just walk away feeling pleased with themselves for protecting the good citizens of Nova Scotia from a dangerous product like ours."

"Do you think we'll really go belly up?"

"I'm sure of it, unless somebody gets them to stop playing this silly game. How do you think the chains will feel if we tell them we can't deliver any product until the inspectors test the yogurt they impounded? It's bound to take longer than they said, even if they do find a test that satisfies them."

"That's true. We'll be history by then," I said, gloomily.

"Oh, and by the way, speaking of outmoded, I happened to glance over Fullerton's shoulder at that book of regulations he was reading from, and I could see it was written back in the early 1990's, so their regulations really are way out of date. They're at least ten years old, if not more. In terms of computer technology, ten years is a century."

"And who do you think writes those regulations? People who have never set foot in a dairy plant the size of ours. They're used to working in big dairy plants, since that's all we have in this country. So their guidelines have nothing to do with a factory like ours. But instead of using their common sense in judging our situation, they just stick to the rules, whether they make sense or not, and *we* have to pay for it."

"Too bad the price has to be so high," Gordon remarked. "I wonder how many other small businesses have fallen by the wayside because of this kind of bureaucratic lunacy."

"It's like the story of David and Goliath, only David doesn't win."

"How *can* he win? When you're small, you have to use a lot of ingenuity in the best of circumstances to win against the big guys. But the bureaucrats are telling us we have to throw our ingenuity out the window and do everything just the way they tell us to do it."

"Imagine telling us we can't use a slingshot! They insist that we use a sword right out of their book of regulations, but we can't kill a giant with a sword in hand-to-hand combat. How are we supposed to defend ourselves if it's against the regulations to use our brains?"

"They don't want us to defend ourselves. They want us out of the picture."

"But, why? They should be *proud* of us! We make them all look good. The tourists talk about that great yogurt they make up here in Canada, as though *Canada* had ownership of it! It's success by association. They're lucky! They ought to take the ball and run with it. What's the matter with them?"

"It's the money, babe. They think big business is good for the economy. They think the big boys have the money to grease the wheels, and maybe some palms, too."

"So they make sure that we can't succeed by regulating us out of having any advantages at all."

"You got it."

"Great. They've tethered Daisy and tied her up in knots. A new twist in an old story. Daisy and Goliath. That's what I'll call my book. *Daisy and Goliath*."

"I like it," Gordon smiled. "Go for it!"

CHAPTER FOURTEEN

The Nightmare Continues

Our yogurt remains impounded

When I explained to Mike Fullerton that these delays would put us out of business, he conferred with his colleagues and came up with this highly implausible suggestion: we would be allowed to continue making yogurt until the tests on the impounded product were completed, providing we took a sample of pasteurized milk from every vat every day to their facility in Truro so that the lab technicians there could determine whether or not it had been successfully pasteurized.

"In other words, not only would somebody have to drive five hours round trip to Truro and back every day, but I'd have to make yogurt 'on spec' until the test results were ready. Is that right?" I asked.

"I suppose so," said Fullerton.

"Okay, then let me ask you this: who is going to have time to drive to Truro every single day of the week? We're all busy here! It's not as though we have nothing to do. We don't have time for this sort of thing, especially since it doesn't make any sense."

"You'll have to decide how to implement our requirements yourself, then. I can't help you with that decision."

"Let me ask you something else then," I said, exasperated. "Where am I supposed to store this yogurt that I'd have to make 'on spec,' now that my entire cooler is filled to the ceiling with a week's worth of yogurt that you've impounded because you think we don't know how to pasteurize our milk?"

"We're trying to work with you, Mrs. Jones. My colleagues and I spent a long time together trying to help you with your problem. But I can't tell you how to run your business. I'm afraid you'll have to figure that out for yourself."

I stared at him. This is what he calls "working" with me? He creates a problem that doesn't exist, then he finds a solution that can't be implemented?

At this point our bewilderment turned to fear and suspicion. When the inspectors refused to release the impounded yogurt *even after receiving a written report from Darose Control* stating that our pasteurization equipment and methods were working correctly *and* we had provided them written records showing the times and temperatures of the milk heating process, it became obvious to us that the federal inspectors were not only being unreasonable, but they appeared to have no intention of allowing us to deliver our yogurt in a timely manner.

They seemed to be casting about in the dark to find some way to prove that their "doubts" had been valid all along. When we asked them, for example, why they were not satisfied with the positive report that was presented to them by Darose Control, they merely stated once again that our method was not acceptable because it was not described in their guidelines. They also reiterated their intention to go to the internet to see if they could find a test that could be done on our yogurt.

Why weren't they satisfied with the usual tests that are performed on yogurt, the ones the provincial inspectors did on a weekly basis? Why did they have to go to the internet to find out how to perform some other tests? Were they not dairy safety inspectors? Did this not include a knowledge of how to test yogurt? Why were they so completely ignorant about how to perform their job? It looked to us as if it had become necessary now for the federal inspectors to save face, and I was afraid they would do everything possible to cast Peninsula Farm in the worst possible light.

We reminded them that the impounded yogurt was getting older by the minute, and that yogurt, unlike cheese or wine, does not improve with age. They remained unconcerned about the problem they had created for us by impounding a storage room filled to capacity with yogurt worth $50,000.00. They were not in the least concerned, either, about the fact that they still had not been able to provide us with a reason for their doubts about our ability to pasteurize milk or for their decision to impound our yogurt.

"There's only one thing to do," I told Fullerton. "We have to find a way to empty out that cooler so we can fill it with new yogurt."

"What do you have in mind?" he asked.

"Well, since you can't find an appropriate way to test the yogurt in the cooler, we'll just have to deliver as much as we can to our client stores in Nova Scotia. I know we can't deliver it interprovincially until you federal inspectors feel satisfied that we know how to pasteurize milk, but the provincial inspectors have never barred us from delivering yogurt here in Nova Scotia, so it looks as though we'll just have to live with reduced sales for a while."

"I'm afraid that's impossible, Mrs. Jones," said Fullerton, after consulting with his colleagues.

"Why not?" I asked. "As far as I know, federal inspectors don't have the authority to stop shipments that remain within provincial borders. Isn't that true?"

"We sat down with the provincial inspectors yesterday, and they all agreed that your yogurt should remain impounded until we find a way of testing it."

"What? Is this agreement legal? The regulations state that dairy products may be delivered provincially without having to be subjected to federal inspection. In other words, provincial inspection is sufficient. So if that's true, it seems to me you're in contravention of the regulations governing the distribution of dairy products in Nova Scotia. And if so, why are you doing this?"

"We're not in contravention of anything, Mrs. Jones. Like I just told you, the provincial inspectors are in complete agreement with us that the yogurt in your refrigerated store room will have to remain impounded till the proper testing has been completed."

"Are they allowed to disagree with you, or do you have the upper hand?"

"Like I said, the provincial inspectors agree unanimously with our decision."

"Okay, then, I have another idea. What about a 'farm gate' sale? We could sell the yogurt on the farm to friends and neighbors. I know for a fact that farm gate sales aren't subject to inspection."

"No, we certainly can't allow you to do that, Mrs. Jones. We're concerned about the safety of your product, whether it is sold in the stores or to people who come to your farm."

I felt myself flush with indignation at his insinuations.

"What if I give it to the hog farmers for pig feed, then?"

"I'm sorry, Mrs. Jones, but we can't let the product off the farm until we are certain that you are pasteurizing your milk successfully. I think I've made that perfectly clear."

"You don't think our yogurt is dangerous to pigs, do you?"

"My concern is that the impounded yogurt could be consumed by humans associated with the pigs," said Fullerton.

The federal inspectors remained determined not to release the yogurt, even though they couldn't explain why they thought something was wrong with it, without any proof that anything was amiss. Our employees were all in favor of the idea of our going ahead and selling it anyway so they could get on with their work, but Gordon and I were the ones who would have to pay the consequences. When I asked the federal inspectors what those consequences might be, I was told they could be anything from a severe fine to a jail sentence.

Our employees were disappointed in us for what they thought was cowardice on our part, but they were not the ones at risk. In fact, our employees were never the ones at risk in any business situation. We always took the blows, and they always got their pay checks. And until the inspectors figured out how to test our yogurt, it looked as though they would get their pay checks that week, too.

Tipping the executioner

"This is beyond belief," said Gordon, as he went through our pile of mail. "Look at this! I've got a bill here from the CFIA wanting me to pay them a registration fee of $895.00 for the honor of inspecting our plant! What kind of a deal as that? They come riding in here like a bunch of cowboys, complaining that we don't know how to pasteurize milk, of all things, and now they want us to *pay* them for coming up with that absurd idea! This whole thing is totally ridiculous. They have no proof, nothing to go on, no reason to accuse us, but they're bound and determined to decapitate us anyway! And to add insult to injury, we have to tip the executioner, just as Mary Queen of Scots did!"

On Monday, June 10th, Mike Fullerton phoned to say that he and his colleagues had finally discovered some specific tests that could be done to determine the presence of E coli, listeria, and salmonella in yogurt. And, he was happy to report, the tests would only take five days.

"E coli!" I exclaimed. "*That's* what you're worried about? But the Department of Agriculture tests our yogurt for E coli every week in Truro, and they've already done it this week on the yogurt you impounded! They told me the results, too. The yogurt is fine!"

Fullerton explained that since he and his colleagues doubted our ability to pasteurize milk successfully, the listeria

and salmonella tests also had to be done, even if the E coli
tests were negative. The inspectors could not be one hundred
percent sure that our yogurt was completely free of all
possible pathogens without doing these specific tests.

So first they make up a problem (we don't know how to
pasteurize milk), and then they demand that we do tests to
determine whether or not the made-up problem is in fact real.
If there had been the slightest reason to assume that there was
anything wrong with our yogurt in the first place, Gordon and
I would have been eager to identify the problem and rectify it
immediately.

But the yogurt on the supermarket shelves was always
available for testing, and should have been tested by the
inspectors before they drew any false conclusions about our
ability to pasteurize milk successfully. Moreover, they should
have taken into consideration the fact that we have never had
any history of making fresh yogurt that caused any problem at
all. Barring that, they should have been satisfied with the tests
that had already been done on the impounded yogurt by the
Department of Agriculture in Truro. But, ironically enough,
they were bound by their own false assumptions to insist on
tests that were rarely conducted, and that would normally only
be done if there were some good reason to believe that the
milk had somehow been contaminated by these unusual
pathogens.

"And who pays the price?" Gordon said. "You got it."

"Plus the tests will take longer than Fullerton claims," I
added. "We both know that E coli takes about five days.
We've seen that from the reports we get from Truro all the
time. But listeria and salmonella are bound to take longer.
I'm pretty sure they'll take two weeks, or maybe more. A
five-day delay in delivering the yogurt is bad enough, but two
weeks! That would be the end of us!"

I decided to call the technician in the microbiology lab
whom I had contacted before, and she assured me that the
listeria and salmonella tests do indeed take at least two weeks.

Shortly after our conversations, Mike Fullerton called and offered to send someone to pick up samples of our yogurt and take them to his lab in Dartmouth for testing. I asked him if he would promise to release the yogurt when the lab results came back negative, but he said he couldn't promise anything until he and his colleagues met to discuss the situation later on, after the test results came back from the lab. He was also unable to tell me when this discussion would take place.

The yogurt hits the fan

When I looked at the calendar I realized that our yogurt would remain impounded for at least two more weeks, until Monday, June 24th. Also, according to Mike Fullerton, there was no guarantee that it would be released even then. What's more, even if the impounded yogurt were released after the two-week testing period, it is a complicated business to pick the orders for over 200 stores and load them all onto the appropriate tractor-trailers.

It takes at least a day to pick the yogurt and another day to load the trucks, which would have taken until Wednesday, June 26th. We could not have been able to start our deliveries until Sunday, June 30th, because our trucks are scheduled to leave the plant on Sundays, so that would be another four days' delay. On top of all that, it takes a full week to deliver the yogurt, bringing the last delivery date to Friday, July 6th.

Any deviation from this normal, carefully worked-out schedule would result in delivery delays and complications that would make it impossible for the truck drivers to finish their job in the allotted time, because once they were off their Sunday departure schedule, they would be off schedule for every single store on their routes. Besides, the receivers at the stores would be very annoyed to see our trucks arriving on the wrong day, causing unexpected delays for the other drivers who were themselves working according to a specific schedule. Many of them would simply send the drivers away.

To sum up the breadth and depth of the problem – if we went along with the inspectors, the total delay for delivering our impounded yogurt would come to four weeks: two for the testing and release of the product, one for picking it and loading the trucks (including waiting for the necessary Sunday start day), and one for delivering the yogurt. Since our company has a policy of removing yogurt from the store shelves one week before the expiry date so that our customers have at least one week to consume it, we would have had to remove the yogurt immediately after we delivered it, if we'd been foolish enough to go along with Fullerton's plan.

I explained all this to the inspectors, but they insisted that there was plenty of time for us to get the yogurt to market should they decide to release it at some future date. They seemed unable or unwilling to grasp the fact that a dairy product that is three or four weeks older than the other brands on the shelf next to it would not appeal to most customers, who would undoubtedly reach for the fresher yogurt.

They also appeared to have no understanding whatsoever of the myriad problems of running a business, and certainly no appreciation for the logistics involved in delivering yogurt to over 200 stores in three provinces – nor were they interested in hearing our explanations. They stubbornly maintained that if the yogurt were delivered some time before the expiry date, everything would be just fine.

"They thought I was exaggerating when I told them it takes a week to deliver yogurt to the stores," I told Gordon. "They couldn't believe it would take two days to pick the yogurt and load the trucks, and they didn't think it was necessary to wait till Sunday before starting our delivery schedule."

"What do *they* know?" he said, sitting down heavily on a kitchen chair and throwing up his hands. "It isn't as though we can just e-mail the yogurt to the stores!"

CHAPTER FIFTEEN

The Hunt for Solutions

A week to fight and regroup

The delays created by the intransigent inspectors would have cost us a minimum of four weeks' worth of product shelf-life, so it no longer made sense to try to deliver the yogurt. It was pointless, therefore, to have Fullerton take it to his laboratory to be tested. Besides, we had by this time lost all confidence that the CFIA was acting in good faith. We had the clear impression that the inspectors were determined to make it impossible for us to conduct business. We would have lost $180,000 in sales during the three-week delay, not to mention the fifty thousand dollars' worth of yogurt that would be standing, undelivered, in the refrigerated storage room at the plant. This was a sum that we couldn't afford to lose and that we would never be able to recuperate.

When it came to the employees, the problem was even worse. We talked to them about whether they would be willing to be laid off for four weeks and go on employment insurance. This immediately raised a hullabaloo from every one of them. They had mortgages to pay, they said. They couldn't wait for weeks and weeks for the first payments to start, they added. The payments were too low, said others, and wouldn't cover their expenses. They would have to look for other jobs anyway if they were on employment insurance, and they'd take a good job any day over having to scrape by on government payments.

This was bad enough from the employees' point of view, but for us the problem of losing our staff was even worse. It's hard enough to train a new employee, because a small company doesn't have people standing around with nothing else to do but train new staff. They all have their own work to do, and when they have to train a new person there are interruptions and delays that can cause mistakes that cost considerable amounts of money. Training two new people is even more difficult, and *three* is well nigh impossible.

The thought of closing down the company while the vat-mounted chart recorders were installed was mind-boggling. More than half our staff told us there was no way they could possibly exist for several weeks on employment insurance. They would have to look for other jobs, and once they got them they certainly wouldn't be coming back. We had over forty people on the payroll, and there was clearly no way in the world that twenty new people could be trained all at one time. The very thought of it was ludicrous. Making yogurt in a home-made fashion is not like slinging hamburgers. It's a craft, and craftsmen need time to develop their skill. The same would be true for an apprenticeship of any kind.

"This has gotten completely out of hand," I said to Gordon. "I think we should just call it quits and shut down the company before we throw good money after bad."

"I hate to throw in the towel, though. I'm not a quitter."

"I know," I said. "I don't want give up, either"

"What do you think we should do, then?"

"Well, first of all, I want to call the inspectors and tell them not to bother to test our yogurt. What's the point? Even *when*, not *if*, it passes their tests, we will have lost more than two hundred thousand dollars, when you count the yogurt in the cooler and add in the lost sales. Besides, most of our employees will have flown the coop. There's no way we'd be able to train a half dozen or a dozen people to take their place, especially not all at one time. Can you imagine trying to do that? It would be totally impossible."

"Well, maybe if we go to a lawyer, or if we go public, or perhaps if we get some politicians involved, we might be able to figure something out. There's *got* to be a solution."

"But time is so vital," I reminded him. "We're bleeding to death financially. We're losing tens of thousands of dollars for every day that goes by."

"Tell me about it."

"So I don't think we could count on the public or even a lawyer to come to our rescue at this point. Lawyers can work at making restitution after the fact, but they can't really stop a crisis in its tracks. As for the public, even if people marched through the streets with signs and clenched fists, they wouldn't be able to change anything quickly enough, if at all."

"Then go ahead and call the inspectors, and tell them not to bother testing the yogurt. It's pointless. Especially when we'd have to shut down anyway to do all the other stuff."

"That's right. We'd be dead in the water. Our only hope is for somebody to tell them to back off and leave us alone."

We began calling everyone we could think of who might take an interest in our plight and who might have the authority to do something to persuade the CFIA to let us continue to produce and distribute our yogurt, at least until such time as they found something wrong with the product. We contacted politicians from all three parties, from members of Parliament to a former premier. All of them were concerned about our situation and were surprised that the federal inspectors had conducted themselves in such a way, especially since they couldn't find anything wrong with our yogurt and had no evidence that our manufacturing procedures were faulty. They all knew, moreover, that we had no history of problems with our fresh yogurt, and nobody had ever been sick. Every one of the politicians offered to do whatever he could to help.

But to their dismay they discovered that they were unable to make any headway at all with the federal inspectors, who countered their pleas by asking them if they would personally accept responsibility for any illness that might occur should they decide to allow us to continue operations. Naturally not one of them felt he was in a position to accept such a weighty responsibility, and indeed they were all absolutely right in their judgment. It was a cruel and unfair question for the inspectors to put to them.

We felt extremely discouraged to learn that the inspectors continued to be as intractable and stubborn as ever, repeating over and over again that they were "only doing their job." If by this they meant their job was to make sure we were driven out of business, they were doing it with admirable proficiency.

We ask for a soft landing

"What are we going to do, Gordon?" I asked, trying to remain calm. "We've always found a way to solve our problems in the past. Why can't we come up with something now?"

"I'll call Ernie Fage. He's the Minister of Agriculture for Nova Scotia. He was a dairy farmer around here for many years. We used to sit on committees together. I'll give him a call and see what he says."

"It's past six o'clock now. Won't his office be closed?"

"I'll call him at home."

His daughter answered, but a few moments later she told Gordon her father was sick and couldn't come to the phone.

"We've been calling so many people, he's probably heard all about what's happening and doesn't want to get involved," said Gordon bitterly.

I finally decided to phone Senator John Buchanan, whom I knew from having sat on the Council on Applied Science and Technology as an adviser to him when he was premier of Nova Scotia. Surely in this one critical moment I could excuse myself for appealing to him for help. I explained to him what had happened and how upset we were about facing the loss of our business as a result of the actions of the CFIA. He promised to do what he could to help, saying that he'd be going to Ottawa the following day and that he'd approach the federal Minister of Agriculture (under whose mandate the federal inspectors operated), to see what could be done. At about 11:00 p.m. Senator Buchanan called us again and told us to phone Ernie Fage, who was awaiting our call.

Gordon delineated the details of the debacle to Ernie, explaining that the worst thing about it was that we were being put out of business as a result of the immediate and future delays caused by the CFIA inspectors. By their actions they had put a complete stop to our income from sales. This created a particularly heavy burden for us because not only did we lack a financial cushion to help us weather the storm, but we were going to be stuck with printed yogurt containers, printed foils, special yogurt cultures, expensive ingredients and many other items that couldn't be sold.

When Ernie asked what he could do, Gordon suggested that, since we were being driven out of business anyway, he might ask the CFIA inspectors if they would please give us 90 days to wrap up our business so that we could use up these materials and enjoy a so-called "soft landing." Ernie said that he thought he could make this idea "fly."

"Gordon, you're a genius," I said, feeling the first ray of hope in a week. "That was an absolutely brilliant idea. If nobody can make the inspectors change their minds, then at least we might be able to save tens of thousands of dollars with your soft landing idea. That would make a *huge* difference. Otherwise I don't know how we're going to pay for all this. It's totally insane!"

The following day, however, Ernie called back to say that the CFIA had rejected the idea out of hand. Once again we got the impression that the federal inspectors were acting in a manner that was capricious, punitive, and without merit. We couldn't help wondering what was behind it all, and whether or not anyone knew the answer to this conundrum.

We spent the rest of the week with our office staff at Peninsula Farm, as we were well aware that the time would come when we'd have to give them the opportunity to look for work elsewhere. They also needed to be given the chance to apply for employment insurance as quickly as possible in case they were unable to find work right away. We had only a few days to figure out where we stood financially before we would lose contact with our former staff.

By the end of the week we realized that our financial situation looked very grim, no matter which way we turned. To attempt to stay in business after losing four weeks' sales worth about $180,000, and then to have to discard our computer system and pay $18,000 and wait several *more* weeks to replace it with equipment that was inferior to what we were already using, was nothing short of absurd. We had very little desire to work with the federal inspectors after they showed themselves to be almost totally unreasonable in every respect. We had no choice but to close the business.

Gordon and I spent the next weekend phoning our staff to inform them that we had been forced by the actions of the CFIA to lay them off and close our doors. It was a heartbreaking job, and it was impossible to explain to any of them why our government would see fit to cause the closure of a local business that provided jobs for rural people at a time when employment was hard to find.

Our employees, however, surprised us and greatly moved us by their generous reactions. After their first shock at hearing the devastating news, most of them expressed concern about *our* future, and their sorrow for the customers who would never again be about to enjoy our products. We will always remember our merchandiser from Port Hawkesbury, who sent us a lottery ticket along with a card expressing her hope that we would win enough money to solve all our problems.

CHAPTER SIXTEEN

Vox Populi

Defamation by innuendo

I t wasn't long before the media caught wind of the closure of Peninsula Farm. Martha Cody of Global TV was the first to cover the news item, then Rick Grant of ATV did another story, and Kelly Cameron of the CBC interviewed us as well. There were articles in the Halifax *Chronicle-Herald, The Bridgewater Bulletin, The Daily News, The Lunenburg Progress Enterprise,* and *Rural Delivery,* as well as radio broadcasts around the province.

The news gave rise to a groundswell of public outrage. We got calls from scores of well-wishers expressing their sorrow at the closure of the company and articulating their disgust with the federal government. Within the next few days we received dozens of sympathetic letters, and the newspapers printed letters from angry citizens everywhere.

We soon learned that the federal inspectors themselves refused (or were not permitted) to talk about the actions they had taken and the decisions they had made. Instead, a man by the name of Freeman Libby, the CFIA agent in charge of western Nova Scotia, quickly stepped up to the plate and assumed the role of spokesman, even though he had never been to our farm or visited the plant. He wasn't even a scientist or a technician, but he didn't mind talking to Martha Cody on Global TV:

We have a mandate to protect the consumer, and at the same time we have another mandate to work with the facility owners to ensure their facility meets the appropriate standards.

I was furious when I heard his statement. First of all, the CFIA was not "working with" the facility owners in any way, shape, or form. On the contrary, they were working against us by impounding our yogurt without cause and by unnecessarily delaying its release. Secondly, Libby did not address the points that the inspectors brought up as constituting their reasons for impounding our yogurt, which were as follows:

1. *They doubted that we were pasteurizing our milk successfully*
2. *They had no proof that the indicating thermometer was accurate.*
3. *They had no proof that our computer recording device was properly calibrated to the indicating thermometer.*

He didn't say why the CFIA doubted that we were pasteurizing our milk successfully. He didn't mention why the inspectors ignored the information provided by the technicians sent by Darose Control Systems stating that our equipment was indeed in good working order. Nor did he or anyone else at the CFIA make any comments about the fact that we heated and held our milk at a temperature and length of time that *far exceeded* their regulations.

Instead, Libby insinuated that we were endangering the consumers, so he was obligated to protect them. He went on to suggest that our facility did not meet the appropriate standards, but he neglected to mention that we had written up an action plan in which we had agreed to make all the changes required by the CFIA during the allotted time frame.

The only items in the inspection report requiring immediate attention involved completing the action report and providing calibration/records for the indicating thermometer, which we did the very next day after the request was made. The other items in the inspection report were not serious enough to require immediate action, nor were they germane to the problem of the impounded yogurt.

The TV viewers, however, were left with the impression that we were not meeting appropriate safety standards. They were also led to believe that our so-called "breech" of these standards was so serious that our yogurt had to be impounded. If that is not defamation by innuendo, I don't know what is.

Libby appeared later that night on a segment of the CBC news. This is how he explained himself to Cynthia Kent:

Questions came up whether or not the safety of the product was there. It's not that I had evidence to say the product wasn't safe, because if I'd had evidence the product wasn't safe then we wouldn't be discussing whether or not it should be released.

The real question here is whether or not the yogurt should have been impounded in the first place. It seems to me that Libby's inspectors would have been well advised to find some evidence that the product wasn't safe *before* jumping to the conclusion that it should be immediately impounded. At least he admits he had no evidence that the product was unsafe, but in the first statement he indulges once again in derogatory hints and insinuations that cast aspersions on Peninsula Farm. He doesn't bother, however, to mention the nature of the questions that "came up" about the safety of the product. Nothing sums up his defamation with vague, meandering statements better than this classic comment, pronounced on an ATV news segment the following night:

Bottom line was that there are standards that have to be met, whether it's a small facility or a large facility, for sanitation and hygienic practices and for ensuring that the product meets an adequate process so it's a safe product.

When the CFIA inspectors came to our plant, nothing was ever said about standards for sanitation and hygienic practices being the reason for impounding our yogurt. The inspectors had not regarded such questions as being of immediate importance, so they had been relegated in the inspection report to a time frame that was to be dealt with in the future. It seemed to us, therefore, that everything Libby said in public was calculated to help him and his inspectors save face for having impounded our yogurt without cause and for having created unconscionable delays. Instead of explaining why the inspectors impounded our yogurt and ignored the technicians' report, Libby simply made equivocal references to sanitation, hygiene, and public safety. His ploy was to win favor with the TV viewers, but nothing he said would have stood up to the scrutiny of anyone who knew the sad facts of the case.

When asked by Gerrie Grevatt of the Halifax *Chronicle-Herald* why he had doubts about our ability to pasteurize our milk successfully, Libby proved himself to be a true master of obfuscation. "There's a difference between having a correct procedure and following the correct procedure," he declared. "We're not saying that the procedure that is laid down as far as the pasteurization process is wrong. What we're saying is there might have been some questions about whether or not the product received the adequate process."

Stuff and nonsense. We not only had excellent, accurate equipment as verified by Darose Control, but we also followed the correct procedure in using that equipment, as proved by the written records generated by our computer system, which was also checked and verified by Darose Control.

On CBC radio's "Maritime Noon," Libby danced around the subject of why he didn't accept the technicians' report by simply denying that he knew anything about it. As the official spokesman for the CFIA, then, he certainly could not have been in very close contact with his inspectors. They had asked me to see to it that a written report was sent to them by the technicians at Darose Control Systems. I did so. The next day I called the inspectors to find out if they had received the report, and they said they had. The only person who knew nothing about the technicians' report was Libby, whose job it was to know the facts and communicate them to the public.

When Costas Halavrezos, the host of "Maritime Noon," asked Libby what he thought about the lengthy delays caused by the inspectors, he replied that we had plenty of time to deliver the yogurt before it expired on July 15th. As usual his information was incomplete and off target. Although our plain yogurt would have expired on July 15th, the code on our fruited yogurt was set for July 8th. As for the smaller containers, we put an even shorter code on them because people tend to put them into lunch boxes, leaving them unrefrigerated for the whole morning. Therefore the 175g tubs were dated for July 1st so the customers would not experience any disappointments.

As for Libby's comment about our having plenty of time to ship our yogurt, I should point out that it's not a question of delivering yogurt before it expires – the idea is to deliver it in a timely fashion so that its dates are similar to those of the other brands on the shelves. Also, the man seemed unaware of the number of days it takes to pick the product, load the trucks, and deliver the yogurt to the stores. Nor did he know how long the tests would have taken. It would seem to me, then, that it is not for him to say whether or not we had plenty of time to ship our product, nor should he presume to make business judgments for people who know far more than he does about such matters.

Libby hinted at certain grave but undefined issues with *Lunenburg Progress Enterprise* reporter Keith Corcoran as well, telling him that "we found what we considered fairly serious problems. We asked until those problems were corrected, that the processing and distribution of the product cease." The provincial inspectors, he added, "were also in agreement with our findings." And yet, amazingly enough, one of those provincial inspectors later told Craig Schrader, our plant manager, that he was free to use the computer logging system if he managed to start up the company again. So much for the "fairly serious problems" that absolutely *had* to be corrected before production could continue.

I rest my case.

Public Outrage

As the days wore on I found myself feeling more and more depressed about what had happened. I couldn't believe such insanity could exist on the face of the earth. I felt outraged that the inspectors had the power to do whatever they pleased to our company, to our employees, and to our customers, and get away with it without giving it a second thought. Like other victims of injustice, I discovered, to my surprise, that I felt ashamed. It was totally irrational, yet the feeling persisted. Maybe I was embarrassed by our failure to defend ourselves from such an ignoble attack. Or perhaps I was humiliated by the fact that we had been trashed by forces so ordinary, so totally commonplace, that their victory became our disgrace. My worst fear was that our customers might be tempted to believe the insinuations that Libby was making. Would they heave a sigh of relief and thank God that we'd been shut down before we had had a chance to poison them with a product that couldn't meet the "high standards" of the federal government?

One individual in particular made me worry about this possibility. He called "Radio Noon" one morning and told the host that he thought people should not romanticize a company just because it's small, local, and well loved by the community. He talked about how fortunate we are to have a government that is prepared to go to any length to protect the safety of the public. By the time he was finished I almost felt as though I should be grateful to the inspectors myself.

What the caller said was true – *of course* we shouldn't put our faith in a company merely because it is small, local, and well loved. We should believe in a company because it has a 25-year track record of making a product that never harmed anyone. We should trust a company whose products are tested regularly and deemed safe by the appropriate government agencies, and whose production methods (although not exactly the same as the ones described in the regulations devised by agribusiness consultants) are nevertheless intelligent, accurate, and perfectly suited to the needs of the small, local, well-loved company in question.

But how was I to get this point across to my customers? I had already been interviewed by the talk show host before the callers began phoning in, so this individual was getting the last word. Would his message stick in the minds of the people?

Would they believe they had been rescued in the nick of time from a potential danger by a kindly, ever-vigilant government? I needn't have worried. The people of Nova Scotia are nobody's fools. Letters from consumers expressing outrage over the closure of Peninsula Farm were printed in newspapers across the province. I took great comfort in reading their intelligent comments, for they proved to me, more than ever before, that our customers appreciated the enormous effort and care that was put into making a product that not only gave them value for their money, but contributed to their health and culinary pleasure as well.

I felt honored that so many people took the time to write to the newspaper editors about the injustice of the situation, but most of all I felt deeply moved by the fact that everyone who wrote letters to the editors were unequivocally on our side. There was no hesitation, no sign of ambivalence or confusion. Barbara Tremills summarized everyone's feelings this way:

Thanks to the Herald for the concise, yet heart-sickening story (June 18) of the closure of Peninsula Farm by the federal health inspection agency.

Too bad we always seem to hear such depressing news after the fact, when all we can do is cry bitterly that once again a small craftsman-like enterprise has been put out of business because it doesn't operate in exactly the same way as a huge conglomerate. We as Nova Scotians are proud of Peninsula Farm's products – the best on the shelves – and are devastated by this heavy-handed, mindless, and destructive action by a federal agency.

Wouldn't you think Big Brother could find the grace to acknowledge that a perfectly good, even superior process, is operating successfully and accept it even though it may not conform to their by-the-book single standard? It's as if the feds were determined to shut down this popular small enterprise (political pressure from the big companies, perhaps?).

I was intrigued that Barbara shared my intuition that the federal inspectors seemed determined from the beginning to put an end to our business, and I was interested to read her opinion that big companies could be behind it all. Anna Taylor, of Blockhouse, picked up on this possibility in her own letter, summarizing her views with the following comments to the editor of the *Chronicle-Herald*:

More and more people are seeking wholesome, fresh, locally produced food. That is why organic farming and organic markets are booming all over Canada and the U.S. This threatens the food giants. And they, in turn, dictate agricultural and health standards.

As one small farmer asked me: "Who are the politicians going to listen to? Me or the guy who contributes $100,000 to his re-election campaign?"

The small farmer's question is certainly a valid one. As chance would have it, I saw Andy Rooney being interviewed on TV that night. "Everybody knows, of course," Rooney said to the host, "that big business and big government are in bed together." Clearly Barbara and Anna and I were not the only ones to make this connection. His words would sound again and again in my mind as I grappled with the question of what had motivated the inspectors. Was there a conspiracy to be found here, or was it, as C. Bailey suggested in his letter to the editor, merely *"a case of some insecure government official justifying his superfluous job just because he can"*?

I found myself leaning toward the conspiracy theory, perhaps because there is more honor in being defeated by an unseen giant than by an insecure government official with a superfluous job and too much undeserved authority. Our downfall, if it was at the hands of such an individual, was only that much more embarrassing.

The truth, however, is almost always elusive and hardly ever what we expect or want it to be. When I made myself choose rationally, and not wishfully, between conspiracy and mediocrity as an explanation for the closure of Peninsula Farm, I found myself leaning in the direction of the latter.

My father, for one, would have heartily agreed. "The world, my darling daughter," he would say in his British accent, "is nothing but one vast desert of *rampant* mediocrity." This pronouncement would always be made with a bulging jugular – he didn't want me to think he was pulling my leg.

I preferred not to jump to any conclusions about the debate going on in my mind, however. The jury was still out. I wasn't sure if I would end up condemning Conspiracy or Mediocrity as the true villain in this drama. Perhaps it was a combination of both, or even something else altogether. The possibilities were well framed in the letter that P.E. Comeau of Comeauville wrote to the Halifax *Chronicle-Herald:*

I've been keeping track of the yogurt debacle. One can speculate about the reasons for the government harassment till the proverbial Peninsula Farm cows come home: bureaucratic autocracy or zealotry; kowtowing to large corporations; a Central Canada bias against Easterners and small town lifestyles, etc. The real reason probably has much to do with the Ottawa bureaucrats being swept up by the prevailing winds of mediocrity that have been fostering the "dumbing down" of nearly everything, and by the fact that they have never tasted the product.

Ever since Peninsula Farm products became available in my region many years ago, the yogurt section in grocery stores has bewildered me. Why would anyone want to buy any other brand? Not only is Peninsula Farm better tasting, but it is also more natural and healthier. Like many others, I don't expect to be switching to other brands.

I'm not a fan of conspiracy theorists, but is the government going to start depriving us of imported cheeses because they aren't as glossy as processed cheese slices? The bureaucrats' Kafkaesque shenanigans are enough to make Easterners cranky at the breakfast table, if not downright cynical.

A succinct summary indeed, and one which asked the same questions that had been bothering me for some time. It was comforting to see that this writer had not come up with any quick or easy answers, but I nurtured the hope that his questions might be of value to me in contributing to the formulation of a better way of doing things where the CFIA is concerned. I can't promise, however, not to become cranky at the breakfast table during the process. Gordon take note.

C. Bailey, whom I quoted previously, also asked the right questions in the paragraph that follows:

When will they (the government officials) realize that small businesses are the backbone of a strong economy, the substance of dreams and a raison d'être for many, as well as an income and alternative to welfare for others? Achievement should be rewarded and encouraged, not crippled with taxes and penalties.

Bailey's almost lyrical phrase, "the substance of dreams and a raison d'être for many," was a beautiful description of the small business, and one that should be incorporated into a statement of purpose for the nation as a whole. For if a business needs a statement of purpose to keep itself going in the right direction, how much more does a great nation need a noble charter to remind its citizens that it's not always all about profit and greed and rampant self-interest?

I chided myself for indulging briefly in some Utopian thinking and perhaps a bit of romanticism as well, which brought to mind the earnest caller who had warned the talk show listeners not to romanticize small, local businesses. The only negative letter in the papers was written by a man who repeated the caller's sentiments (could the caller and the writer have been one and the same man?). When I saw his name it didn't take me long to find out just who this lone dissenter was: he was a medical doctor on the government's payroll.

CHAPTER SEVENTEEN

Best Before

The tests results come in

B y the third week of the ongoing fiasco I found the time to turn my attention to the yogurt samples we had stored in our refrigerator after the lab technicians told us they could not perform the tests requested by the CFIA (the federal inspectors at that time had not yet figured out what tests to ask for). Gordon and I decided to drop the samples off at Philip Analytical Services Inc to have them tested anyway.

We looked forward to framing the test results and hanging them on the wall. We wanted to tell our grandchildren some day all about the federal inspectors and their pathetically fruitless efforts to find something wrong with our yogurt. We wanted them to know how the government first encouraged, then destroyed, one of the few local companies that had ever stood up to the multinationals for even a short time, let alone for twenty-five years.

We received a telephone call the following week from a lab technician from Philip Analytical, informing us that the test results were ready. We were surprised that they were available so soon, for we had been told that although E coli takes a week, tests for listeria and salmonella take two weeks to complete. But Annette, the microbiologist in charge of the testing, said that the samples were so clean there was no point in waiting any longer.

"There wasn't a trace of listeria or salmonella to be found," she said. "It would have been a waste of time to let the samples keep on incubating in the test lab. Nothing can grow from nothing, as you can imagine. But we were surprised. I mean, usually when we get samples for testing, we find all sorts of bugs crawling around. After all, people generally have a reason for suspecting there's some kind of contamination, or they wouldn't pay to have their products tested."

"It was expensive, was it?" I said.

"Well, it's a lot of work for us. You know how it goes. You have to wait around a long time to watch the organisms grow, and labor is costly. But your tests won't be expensive, because we didn't have to wait very long at all to figure out that nothing was going to grow, no matter how long we waited. I guess it was pretty much a waste of time, but I'm sure you're happy with the results. The thing is," she continued, "we haven't seen clean samples like yours in a long time. "What made you think there was something wrong with them, anyway?"

What indeed?

I asked Annette if the presence or absence of pathogens in yogurt could prove whether the milk had been pasteurized correctly or not. She said that test results on yogurt did not prove anything about pasteurization. If pathogens were present in the yogurt they could have entered after pasteurization. If pathogens were not present in the yogurt it might only mean they were not present in the milk in the first place.

"It's just common sense," she added.

The steam was coming out of my ears. It was exactly as I thought. A tempest in a teapot, but a tempest all the same, with all its devastating effects. And yet, unlike other storms, this one could have been completely avoided if the inspectors had had the slightest interest in really "working with us," as they so often claimed they were trying to do.

Gordon was pleased, but not surprised, when I told him about the results. The anger, though, was not long in coming.

"They've put us through all this for absolutely nothing!" he said, raising his voice. "Why couldn't they have retested the yogurt that was already on the store shelves? Why did they insist on impounding the yogurt we were packaging on the week of the inspection? Why didn't they accept the tests that had already been done by the Department of Agriculture on the yogurt they impounded? Why did they impound the yogurt just because our computer system wasn't in their guidelines? What set them up to it? Who was behind it?"

"I'm afraid we'll never know," I said, feeling depressed. "Sometimes I think that the most probable explanation is the easiest one... they were scared they might be held responsible if our yogurt ever hurt anyone at any future date, so to protect themselves they followed their regulations to the absolute letter."

"Don't tell me about the letter of the law," Gordon almost shouted. "I only want to know about the *spirit* of the law."

"Yes, and the spirit of the law can get you into a whole lot of trouble. Just ask any lawyer."

"Those inspectors are cowards, there's no other way to put it," Gordon said bitterly. "Why couldn't they see that our way of making yogurt was every bit as good, if not better, than the method described in their regulations?"

"They probably did see it. But they knew that if they followed the regulations, nobody could find fault with them. They'd be completely blameless if anything went wrong with our yogurt and they ended up in court."

"So they prefer to import yogurt that's been inspected *somewhere else*? Isn't that even more risky for the people of Nova Scotia? Who knows what kind of testing they do in other places? That way we're bound to lose control over the safety of our own food."

"Yes, but at least the responsibility is on somebody else's shoulders. That's all they care about."

"All right, if that's the way they want it," Gordon growled. "But don't let me hear them making any more statements in the media about how deeply they care about the people of Nova Scotia. It's downright pathetic."

"That's the trouble with all of us, I guess. We want to buy insurance for everything – especially insurance against having to accept responsibility of any kind."

"But there has to be a limit," said Gordon, flaring up again. "How can anybody promise other people that they'll be a hundred per cent safe? And who would want to be that safe, anyway? How on earth would businesses develop and grow if entrepreneurs didn't take risks? And how would artists ever create anything new or lasting if they didn't take risks? Life isn't all about safety nets. There's no perfect safety in this world for anyone."

"Least of all for entrepreneurs who dare to be different."

"Touché," Gordon said, glumly.

Bruce MacKinnon, the talented cartoonist whose drawings appear daily in *The Halifax Chronicle-Herald,* captured the absurdity of our situation with brilliant accuracy. He drew a cartoon of a Peninsula Farm yogurt container squashed by a giant hand grasping a code date stamp. Yogurt was spilling out everywhere. The plastic yogurt container had been completely destroyed. And there, on the bottom of the container where the expiry date was supposed to be, were the words, "Best before... government interference."

We couldn't have said it better ourselves.

Fitness versus variety

There are good people in this world. When word got out that we had been forced to close the company, friends and strangers alike came forward to give us whatever help they could. They were willing to write letters, make phone calls, and get on the net. Some people even offered to lend us money or raise money for us – a gesture which moved us greatly.

Others wanted to buy the company, certain that if Gordon and I remained in the picture as consultants, they would be able to make a success of it. We didn't relish the idea, however, of trying to run a company by standing in the wings and watching other people flounder. It had taken us twenty-five years and many costly errors to get to the point where we could manage to run Peninsula Farm ourselves, but we had started out in kinder times, long before the advent of multinationals and cut-throat competition.

Still others wanted us to pay them to be *our* consultants, thinking they could rescue the company by providing us the management skills they must have thought we lacked. A few venture capitalists also came around and sniffed the air, but they were quickly convinced that the company was unlikely to give them enough profit on their investment.

It wasn't a matter of money, however. It was a matter of a small company that had slowly evolved from nothing, surviving in spite of its predators, and not easily duplicated. It had died without progeny, and because it was unique, it was now extinct. It wasn't money that was needed to save the company, although money is always useful. What was needed was an appreciation for its special beauty. What was needed was the kind of love that Jane Goodall had for her chimps, or that Dian Fossey had for her mountain gorillas. What was needed was a respect for others that doesn't demand insurance coverage for oneself. The final chapter on the well-being of chimpanzees and gorillas has yet to be written, to be sure, but it is widely accepted that their most dangerous predators are humans.

"It's a dog eat dog world," proclaimed one of the vulture capitalists who was circling around our dying company. "If you can't compete, then you don't deserve to be alive," he added, with obvious self-satisfaction. "It's the survival of the fittest, you know. That's what life is all about."

This, of course, is exactly the philosophy that underlies globalization and which is responsible for so much extinction of one kind or another. I once asked a government think tank to consider the idea of putting tariffs on yogurt shipped to Nova Scotia from Ontario and Quebec, since they had almost all the advantages and we had next to none. Both provinces were able to sell their yogurt down here at a lower price than ours, partly because Ontario has a large population at its doorstep, and Quebec has the lion's share of the milk quota. We, on the other hand, were left with the job of having to find room for their plastic yogurt containers in our garbage dumps. Shouldn't we at least be charging them something for these inconveniences, so that we might have a fighting chance to stay alive down here in the Maritimes?

"There's a word for that, Mrs. Jones," remarked one of the thinkers in the tank. "It's called *protectionism*. Now, if we want to make progress as a nation and get ahead in the world, we don't want to start by protecting the companies that don't know how to compete. If you're too small to handle the big boys out there, Mrs. Jones, then I'm afraid you might want to look for another line of work. You should stick to what you do best. Play to your strengths, you know what I'm saying? Now, I've heard you're a very fine Spanish professor..."

He reminded me of the editor from Doubleday who stood in my kitchen that day, saying the very same thing – I should just stick to making ice-cream. I contemplated my friend the thinker, wondering to what lengths I would have to go to persuade him that his "survival of the fittest" theory was all right for the "big boys," but that my little company represented the natural variety that is an important part of the business ecology. Put all your eggs into one basket, and there's trouble when disaster strikes. That holds true for eggheads in a think tank, too.

Can Daisy rise like a Phoenix from the ashes?

When it came to the kind of love that Jane Goodall and Dian Fossey felt for the vulnerable primates of the African jungle,

Blair Landry had distinguished himself among our employees for his loyal, protective affection for Peninsula Farm. At one time in the past, when Gordon and I were feeling particularly old and weary, Blair stepped bravely forward and offered to buy the company.

Of all the employees we had on the payroll, Blair had the most experience with every aspect of the business. He had started with us when he was only a teenager, and had eventually become proficient in the areas of plant management, quality control, distribution, merchandising, marketing, demonstrations, advertising and sales. He was also good at doing cost/benefit analyses, having majored in statistics at Dalhousie, and he was quick to catch on to other aspects of the business that required a knowledge of finance. He was adventurous, personable, and more than willing to take on the most difficult and unenviable tasks without hesitation. He was a born leader, an unwavering optimist, and fun to have around.

At that time in our lives we lived in fear of the day when he would tell us that he had found a job with a larger company that could afford to pay him a higher salary. But to our great relief, that day would be delayed for a long time to come. Blair had the maturity and insight to understand that it was precisely because we were a small company that he was able to enjoy such a wide variety of business experiences. So he came to us that day and offered to buy the business if we could help him put together some sort of a financial package that would allow him to swing the deal. We were proud of him for having both heart and gumption, and we decided to do what we could to help out.

If anyone on our staff could manage to operate the business, that person was certainly Blair. Our girls were out of the house and gone – one was studying art in Michigan, and the other was a medical student in New York. Blair was the sole heir when it came to handing down the business to someone willing and able to keep it alive. Accordingly, Gordon approached a private firm whose function was to invest union pension funds in promising Canadian companies. The firm was a mutual fund that had the benefit of some tax relief because it helped create jobs for local people, particularly in rural areas.

It turned out that the group was interested in helping Blair buy Peninsula Farm, but he couldn't quite swing it on his own. We were unable to contribute our retirement savings to this arrangement, since neither Gordon nor I had a pension to fall back on. Blair, in spite of his risk-taking nature, was unwilling to mortgage his house to buy the company, largely because he was now married and expecting a child soon, so this necessarily colored his views and those of his bride.

He tried to convince a number of the other employees to make it a group effort, but his colleagues were either too young or too nervous to fall in step. And so the plan fell through, and Gordon and I kept soldiering on. The truth is, we were glad to have a continuing source of income so that we could contribute to our daughters' education, which was, we felt, an important investment in their future.

Meanwhile Craig, who was little more than a teenager at the time that Blair was considering the purchase of our business, had now grown older and was hoping to buy Peninsula Farm after the federal inspectors forced us to close. By this time Blair had three children and had become the manager of a prominent trucking company, so Craig was eager to step into his buddy's shoes.

He wasn't as outgoing as Blair, and he didn't have the same leadership qualities, but he was a good plant manager and quite capable of building a new plant himself. He was clever with figures and shrewd about cost control, so within a few days he presented us with a proposal to buy the company. The purchase figure itself was low, but we were not in a position to be choosy. Besides, we loved the idea of having the company end up in the hands of an employee.

The provincial government took a serious look at Craig's proposal, but soon realized that he didn't have enough personal credit to fund a new start-up on his own.

"We would be pleased to reconsider the application if you and Mrs. Jones provide the necessary funding," said one of the government loan officers to Gordon. "But you can't just lend Mr. Schrader the start-up funds," he added. "The new owners, whoever they end up being, would have to prove to us that they had sufficient capital to see the project through."

We were in no position to provide anyone with any capital whatsoever. We had not yet thoroughly assessed the damages, but we quickly calculated that we would have little in the way of personal assets once we paid our creditors.

"It's ironic, isn't it?" I said to Gordon later that day. "First the government comes along and puts us out of business, then they offer to lend us the money to get back into business again. They made this whole fiasco cost as much as possible. They wouldn't give us a soft landing or bend their regulations to suit our situation. And now they want us to cough up *more* money into the bargain. How would *they* like to face retirement with a mountain of debt on their hands? It's not as though we were young people just starting out."

"We're dealing with different branches of the government," said Gordon. "The provincial lending agency doesn't care what kind of damage the feds have caused in our case. They just want to do their own job, which is to lend money to people who don't need it, and not lend it to anyone who does. So that puts Craig out of the running."

"It looks as though Craig was Peninsula Farm's last hope," Gordon said sadly. "But in a way, I'm just as glad he won't have to deal with all the headaches and heartaches of running a medium size company in this new business climate. Perhaps at this point the best thing is to keep family businesses as small as possible. Neighbors helping neighbors, but flying well under the radar. Once you go head-to-head with the big corporations, you can pretty well kiss your future goodbye. Survival of the fittest. Hah!"

"You know, I've always believed that the dinosaurs died when the ice age came because they couldn't find any way of staying warm. Only the smallest creatures survived, little furry mammals and the like, because they could make burrows or find shelter for themselves under a dead branch, or whatever. So if an ice age hits the business world, it may turn out that the fittest companies for survival will be the smallest ones of all, not the multinational conglomerates, as everyone seems to believe. It would be ironic, wouldn't it?"

Neighbors helping neighbors. The infrastructure was already in place, as friends and total strangers contacted us in the days that followed our closure to ask if they could lend us money or put on a drive to raise money to keep us in business. Although we were grateful for their offers and touched by their willingness to help, our dealings with the government lending agency made it abundantly clear to us that it would be wrong to accept any help from outside sources, since there really needs to be a solid, dependable, ongoing cash flow before a new business start-up can even be considered. All we knew was that our own cash cow had been milked completely dry.

CHAPTER EIGHTEEN

The End of the Line

Peninsula Farm is history

It was one of those dismal Nova Scotia mornings where fog blows in from the ocean and covers the land with a sense of doom. It was the kind of day that farmers dread, when cut hay lies wet as noodles on the moist land. I had chosen a bad day to do the books.

"We've come to the end of the line," I said to Gordon that morning. "Do you think we should declare bankruptcy? Isn't that what businesses do when they get wiped out?"

"It's certainly worth seeing a lawyer about it. I think we need professional advice before we go any further."

After sitting down with our Halifax lawyer and explaining to him what had happened to us, he recommended that we go to a trustee in bankruptcy procedures and tell him the whole story all over again.

The bankruptcy trustee was eager to take our case, and did his best to convince us that we should leave everything in his singularly expert hands.

"Too many owners think they can handle the liquidation of a business all by themselves," he said, folding those competent hands neatly on the table. "But they have no idea what it's really going to be like. People can be nasty when you owe them money. All the polite talk you used to get from the service sector goes right down the drain. That can be a devastating wake-up call. I've known owners who ended up with nervous breakdowns. They thought they had friends, and in no time flat these so-called friends turn into enemies, and it gets up close and personal. I advise you not to subject yourselves to that."

The bankruptcy trustee's soothing words had the expected effect. Nobody wants to let down a tradesman who has loyally provided goods and services for over twenty-five years. In a small town these people are generally personal friends, and it's painful to have to explain that there's going to be a little trouble with the final payments. It was hard to believe, however, that friends who had made good money from dealing with us for so many years would really be that upset about not making a profit on the final bill.

"You don't know human nature," the bankruptcy trustee said. "It's better to let a professional handle it. At least that way everyone knows they're being treated the same way."

"It'll be a lot of work for you," I replied. "Where are we going to find the money to pay you?"

"You don't have to pay me a cent," he replied. "That's the beauty of it. Your creditors will pay me, whether they like it or not. They'll take the rap for the whole thing."

"What do you mean? How does that work?"

"I come to your place and I set up an asset sale, then I give your creditors whatever is left over after I pay myself for my services. It's as simple as that."

"And how much would our creditors get?" Gordon asked.

"That depends on how much I can get for your assets, and how much you owe your creditors."

After studying our financial statements, the bankruptcy trustee figured he could get about $150,000 for the factory equipment. Then, after paying himself for his services, he'd be able to give our creditors about five cents on the dollar.

"That's it? Only five cents on the dollar?" I exclaimed.

"That's actually very good," said the bankruptcy trustee. "Most creditors end up with nothing at all in these cases. You ought to know that yourself. Haven't you ever been stung?"

We had, indeed, been stung a number of times. Small operators would go out of business and never pay their final bills. Some would even abscond with equipment we had lent them, such as coolers or freezers, but we knew it was useless to press the issue with small business operators who had nothing left to show for their effort but disappointment and hurt pride. We always tried to keep in mind that the business relationship had obviously been more profitable for us than it had been for them, since they, and not we, were the ones who were going belly up, so we would just write off their failures as the cost of doing business.

It was hard to believe that this wouldn't be abundantly clear to our own creditors, now that our turn had come. Surely they wouldn't try to kick us when we were down. We knew them too well. We had dealt with them for many years. Would we really go to the brink of a nervous breakdown if we tried to handle the situation ourselves? The bankruptcy trustee claimed that he was only trying to protect us from having to go through the misery of dealing with our creditors. But why on earth should we declare bankruptcy and let the trustee get the lion's share of the asset sale, when it seemed only right that the creditors themselves should be getting his portion?

"Sonia and I have talked it over," Gordon informed the bankruptcy trustee the next day. "We've decided to handle the closure of the business ourselves."

"Fine by me," the trustee said. "But if you run into trouble and you think you can't take it any more, I'll be here for you. Don't hesitate to call."

We pay off our creditors

Once I had a final list of exactly what we owed our creditors, I got on the phone and started the laborious process of calling them up one by one to tell them that we had decided to close the business rather than declare bankruptcy.

"We looked at the options," I said, "and we found that if we filed for protection under Chapter Eleven, the bankruptcy trustee would give you maybe five cents on the dollar. But if we simply stop operations and close down right now, we can give everyone fifty cents on the dollar. So we figured it was pretty much a no-brainer. In a perfect world we would have paid you off in full, but this way at least we can give you enough to cover your costs, so you won't be losing very much when we send you the final payment."

Most people were very happy to get fifty cents on what was still owing to them after we had returned any unused ingredients that could be resold by their companies (the bankruptcy trustee told me later that he would have sold the unused goods at full value to someone else and pocketed the cash, and *then* he would have paid the creditors fifty cents – a "clever" business tactic).

Many of our customers must have been burned in the past by people going bankrupt, for they were gracious enough to thank us for taking the time and the trouble to close down the business ourselves rather than just handing it over to a bankruptcy trustee. They were satisfied to sign a release paper stating that they accepted our offer and would not seek further reimbursement of moneys owing. One or two of our creditors, however, were less than pleased with the arrangement.

"I opened up that there well," said a local plumber angrily, "and I put the pump down it, and I want to get paid for everything you owe me. If you don't pay me in full," he added, "I'm going to send my men over there to your farm and they'll dig up the well and haul that pump away."

I told him he was welcome to come and take the pump away, and that I was very sorry we couldn't pay him in full, especially since it was a relatively small amount. But if I paid some creditors more than others, I explained, it would not only be unfair, but the whole group of them would have every reason to seek recourse from the law. Then I'd have to go bankrupt for sure, and everyone would end up with five cents after all.

"All I want is for you to pay me what you owe me," he said. "I installed that pump for you, and you owe me for the work I done. I work hard for a living."

"I understand, and I respect that. All I can say is I'm truly sorry about the pump. I wish all this had never happened. I feel the same way you do about it. I know what hard work is."

"Yeah, I know," he said, his voice softening. "I seen you out in the fields hoistin' bales of hay, and drivin' them trucks down the highway. It makes me mad, though, that us hard-workin' guys never gets a break. Me *and* you, I'm sayin'."

The only other creditor who was disappointed with the arrangement at that time was a large corporation to whom we owed a considerable sum of money for some equipment we had bought from them. They were unimpressed with my offer of fifty cents on the dollar.

"We don't accept partial payments, Mrs. Jones," the person in charge of accounts receivable informed me. "It's company policy. We'll work with you, though. We'll give you some extra time to come up with the money. But that's about the best we can do for you."

"Well, unfortunately it won't matter how much time you give me," I told him. "The business is closed, so there won't be any more money coming in. And we've already exhausted our personal savings. I'm really sorry I can't pay you in full, but I don't see how the situation will improve with time."

"I'll have to pass this on to our company's lawyers, then," he sighed. "This will have to be decided by a judge."

Fortunately it didn't end up in the courts after all. But one angry creditor almost managed to haul us before a judge for payments owing on the last shipment of certain ingredients we had received at the farm. I didn't even know that the ABC Corporation had filed a lawsuit against me until a reporter called to ask me how I felt about the situation.

"What? They're *suing* us? But they already told me on the phone that they would sign my release paper. They agreed to go along with the offer I've made to all my other creditors."

"Did you get it in writing?" the reporter asked.

"No, but they said they'd put it in the mail right away. It's true I haven't received it yet, but if they changed their minds about it, why wouldn't they call me back and discuss it with me? Why would they suddenly turn around and *sue* me without a word of warning?"

The reporter didn't answer. He was too busy taking notes for his story.

As soon as I got off the phone with him I called the ABC Corporation and tried to talk to the executive who had promised to sign the release papers, but he wasn't available. Every time I called from then on I was told that he was away from his desk, or on a long distance call, or out of the office, or in one of the endless meetings that are always in progress whenever a person wants to dodge what he considers to be a nuisance call. It made me angry to think that this man was avoiding me after I had bought several million dollars worth of ingredients from him over the years, at what must have been a very reasonable profit for him. Now that I was asking for some latitude on the final payment (the only one owing on approximately 150 shipments), he saw fit to make himself unavailable.

The next day, while I was in our Halifax apartment, I was surprised to hear someone buzz at the front entrance downstairs. It was unusual for people to stop by without calling first to make sure their visit was convenient. When the business was still functioning I used to spend a great deal of time in my kitchen developing and refining new products, but my friends knew that I preferred not to be disturbed while the experiments were in progress.

I decided not to answer the buzzer. The reporter's words were too fresh in my mind. I wasn't ready to have anyone thrust a court summons at me until I had a chance to clear things up with the executive at ABC who had promised to accept my offer of fifty cents on the dollar. I sat quietly at my computer, hoping the person who had buzzed would assume nobody was home. If it did turn out to be a friend who was just passing by, she would no doubt call me later.

The next thing I knew, I heard a knock on my apartment door. That was even *more* unusual. Solicitors weren't allowed to roam the halls, so the only person who would ever knock would be someone living in the building, and that was fairly rare. Even the supers called first before knocking on the door.

I crept up to the peephole and saw a bull-necked man in an ill-fitting suit and tie standing in the hall with a briefcase in his hand. He looked to me like the sort of person who made it his business to seek and find citizens cowering in their apartments, and his briefcase seemed to be bulging with process papers just waiting to be served. I sneaked back to my computer and went on with my work, hoping he'd go away.

"Murray, please don't let anyone in if they tell you they want to see me," I said to the super when the coast was clear. "Most of them are just trying to sell me something, and I'd rather avoid them."

"I never saw nobody come up here," Murray said. "He must have got in behind someone else."

"It's okay. But next time, could you just tell them I'm in a meeting or something? Please?"

"No problem," said Murray.

To my astonishment there came another knock on the apartment door five minutes later. Was it Murray? Had he forgotten to tell me something? I looked through the peephole and saw the process server standing there again. He was still in the building! Where had he been hiding when I was talking to Murray? In the stairwell? Maybe he had left the building and then come back to try once more, but how had he slipped past Murray again?

I hated being trapped in my apartment while he waited in the hall. The man was a bull dog. Fortunately we had a double apartment with a different number on each door. It occurred to me that if I left the apartment through the back door, the man waiting outside would probably not realize it was me. So out I went through the kitchen door and brazenly called the elevator as though I were the neighbor lady. The bull dog gave me a sideward glance, but paid little attention as I stood there waiting for the elevator to arrive. As the elevator doors closed behind me, I heard him rapping loudly again at the front door of our apartment.

I greeted Gordon that evening when he came back from Lunenburg, bubbling with the story of how I had avoided the process server.

"The longer I put off having to establish a court date," I explained, "the more time we'll have to try to come to an understanding with ABC. So, are you proud of me? I bought us some extra time!"

"Proud of you?" he said, breaking into a smile and shaking his head. "I don't exactly know how to answer that question. The poor man got so tired of trying to find you home that he eventually drove all the way to Lunenburg to talk to me instead."

"What?" I cried, horrified at what I was hearing. "You let him in? Did he serve you the papers? Did you sign them?"

"He gave me the papers, and I signed them. Yes."

"But Gordon, now we're going to get hauled into court before I have a chance to talk to the man who wants to sue us! He's been dodging my calls for two days now, so I was going to drop by and pay him a surprise visit. I was sure I could get him to come around if I just talked to him. But now it's too late. You've signed the process server's papers!"

"What? You thought he was a *process server?*" He looked at me and suddenly burst into laughter.

"Well, what's so funny?" I asked impatiently.

"He wasn't a process server," said Gordon, trying his best to stifle his laughter. "He was the executive from ABC, the one you've been trying to get in touch with all this time. He wanted to hand-deliver the release paper you sent him to sign. ABC agreed to take fifty cents on the dollar, and they were just trying to clear it up as quickly as possible. They're withdrawing their lawsuit. I think it's all the bad publicity they've been getting."

CHAPTER NINETEEN

Shattered Dreams

Cleaning up the mess

There's something gratifying about cleaning the house, or weeding the vegetable garden, or reorganizing the file cabinets. When the work is done you can enjoy the results. But there was nothing gratifying about cleaning up the mess that was left by the closure of Peninsula Farm. Gone was the sound of trucks beeping as they backed up to the loading dock, gone were the voices of the office workers talking on the phones, gone was the cheerful clanking of machinery in the factory, all of which once indicated that work was being done, bills were being paid, and paychecks were being prepared.

Instead, Gordon and I worked all alone in an empty office, struggling to find documents whose location was known only to the employees who had been responsible for them in the past. This was the most aggravating work we had ever done, and there was no paycheck to look forward to, either. The worst of it was that the clean-up took much longer than we had expected. Weeks dragged into months, and finally a whole year went by before we could say that our thankless job was almost done.

The clean-up process had begun shortly after the decision was made to close down Peninsula Farm, when we were faced with the problem of what to do with the yogurt that had been locked into our walk-in cooler. We decided to ask Rick Joudrey, our licensed, certified, in-house diesel truck and refrigeration maintenance man, to stoop to the job of hauling the yogurt to the town dump. He and a couple of other soon-to-be laid off plant workers loaded two trailers with the fresh and frozen product, and off they went down the road to the Lunenburg recycling plant. Cheryl Lohnes, a book-keeper on our payroll for over ten years and a talented photographer, snapped pictures of the event as it unfolded. It sickened me to see our yogurt wasted in such an appalling fashion.

"You should have seen them guys at the dump," said Rick, when he got back to the farm. "Women, too. They came from all over, with boxes and carts and anything they could carry, and they loaded it all up and drug it home."

I was delighted to hear that our customers still had perfect confidence in our product, in spite of the insinuations of the CFIA. The voice of the people quickly made itself known in the pages of the local newspapers, too. Cheryl Devine, from Barrington Passage, had this to say:

Peninsula Farm yogurt is a superior product. Astro, Danone, and the other big outfits do not come close to Daisy's product. Having $50,000 worth of delicious yogurt dumped in a landfill marked the end of a wonderful family business started in Sonia Jones's kitchen. (By the way, my family would gladly have taken at least 20 liters of that product and gobbled it up in a week. We've been eating it for the past 20 years.) 'Tis a sad day, indeed, when the locks were put on Daisy's operation. We're truly sad to see you leave our grocery shelves; you'll be missed.

The end came, as far as I was concerned, in a very tangible way and on a specific day that I'll never forget. We were trying to make the farm look as attractive as possible so we could put it up for sale. We had both agreed that the smaller additions to the yogurt factory should be torn down and hauled away, leaving the original building in place to be used as the new owners saw fit. We contracted a company to send a team over with heavy equipment to do the deed. It took them only one morning to rip everything apart, creating a pile of rubble so high that it completely concealed the remaining building.

I stood at our bedroom window and looked down on the wreckage. And then I lost it. It seemed to me that the massive pile of debris symbolized our lives. It had all been for naught. Gordon and I had wasted our time.

That's what a pile of shattered dreams looks like. What's the use of trying? How could I ever again face a room full of young people and give them a pep talk about making it on their own? Who cares, anyway? Why bother?

"There you are!" Gordon sang out. "I was looking everywhere for you. What are you doing up here, sitting in the bedroom? The wreckers want to be paid."

"Great. Let's pay the wreckers, by all means. Let's give them our *blood,*" I said, the tears streaming down. "Let them take everything. Let them haul me away with the rest of the rubble. Let them take me to the dump!"

"They'll have all that junk gone by tomorrow morning," said Gordon, helpfully. "You don't have to be so dramatic."

"Dramatic! You call this *dramatic?*" I said, rousing myself into a state of furious resentment against Gordon for not sharing the moment or understanding my anger and grief. I wanted him to hug me, and reassure me, and give me some words of wisdom.

"Do you know where the checkbook is?" he asked. "The guys want to go to lunch. They're waiting."

"No, I don't know where the checkbook is. I don't know, and I don't care. Give them *my* lunch, if they're so hungry. I never want to eat again."

Gordon made a frustrated grunt and left the room. I wallowed in my misery a bit longer, till my eyes were burning and there were no more tears. It dawned on me that he had unwittingly done me a favor in turning my tears to anger. I was mad enough to get up and walk away from my despair.

I got downstairs just as he was coming back to the house. His face was smudged and stubbly and his hair was spiky with sweat, but he was surprisingly handsome for a man of seventy-two. He was still rugged, and he had no belly overhang. I was a lucky woman. I wondered if other women eyed him once in a while. I was surprised I couldn't answer that question.

"There, that's all taken care of," he said. "I paid the guys, so now I can take you to lunch."

Gordon is a one-thing-at-a-time sort of man, so once he had sent the wreckers on their way and we were comfortably settled in a booth at Magnolia's, he was able to concentrate his full attention on my fading feelings of depression.

"I didn't mean to minimize anything," he said, spreading rhubarb sauce on his fishcakes. "You have every right to feel blue. We both do. But it's over now, and we have to move on. We have to think about the future. You should get going on that book of yours. We can share our experiences with other people, and maybe some good will come of it."

That was the turning point, our lunch at Magnolia's. Gordon helped me realize that soldiering on is not such a bad idea. At that moment, however, I felt too depleted to imagine expending the energy necessary to write another book. But I knew the time would come, perhaps in a lovely seaside village in a southern clime, when the muse would visit me once again. I just hoped I wouldn't have to sequester another editor before the new book saw the light of day.

Bureaucratic vandalism

Once the creditors were paid off and the mess was cleaned up, the time finally came for us to attempt to make sense of the calamity that had befallen us. Gordon and I had many discussions about the disastrous effects of globalization, about job loss through outsourcing, and how the poor are getting poorer while the rich get richer. We talked about the erosion of democracy as money and influence put unelected corporate CEO's in positions of unheard-of power, and we spoke about the effects of unbridled greed leading to despair on the part of many. The world was beginning to look grim indeed.

In our effort to understand the "why" and the "wherefore" of our situation and how it fit into the new developments in the world, I reread an article by Charles Moore called "Bureaucratic vandalism" that had appeared in the Halifax *Daily News* not long after our debacle with the federal inspectors. He had this to say about the role of bureaucracy in the closure of Peninsula Farm:

It's a truism that bureaucracy is synonymous with the most bone-headed and obtuse sort of stupidity. One can still hope that's an exaggeration, but there's plenty of evidence that it's not... It's probably not fair to blame the local CFIA officials, who don't make the rules, and are just doing their jobs at the bidding of their bosses in Ottawa. However, it's fair to blame the technocratic, bureaucratic mentality behind the brain-dead regulations. The CFIA argues that the standards must apply to all food products and may not be deviated from.

"It doesn't matter if you have a large plant or a small plant, you have to treat food the same way," one official explained.

Well, that may be the regulations, but if so, they're idiotic and ought to be changed. For that matter, the entire mentality behind the food regulation "apparat" in this country needs changing. Obviously, some sort of food-safety regulatory structure is necessary, but there is something badly out of whack when that structure smiles benignly – even promotes – the use of chemical additives in food, antibiotics and growth hormones in animal agriculture, pesticides and chemical fertilizers in fruit and produce production, but puts cottage-industry producers out of business because they don't use standard, arguably inferior and ill-suited production methods. Especially in the absence of any complaints or evidence of safety problems with the product.

Since the closure of Peninsula Farm, we received many phone calls from other small business owners wanting to share their own experiences with "excess regulatory foolishness" (to quote Charles Moore). There were many stories about food manufacturers running afoul of the CFIA for incomprehensible reasons. It seemed clear to me that the inspectors applied the regulations with no thought to the cost or the time involved with instituting the changes they demanded.

Marg Hennigar, editor of the Bridgewater *Bulletin* and the Lunenburg *Progress Enterprise*, was aware of the problems created by regulatory inflexibility. She had this to say in her article entitled "Terrorism, Canadian style":

Unquestionably, governments have to monitor and regulate food production and manufacturing. Surely, however, they could add some common sense to the exercise and not encourage power-hungry bureaucrats to turn regulations against the people they hire them to protect.

After describing the irrationality of the inspectors' decision which led to the closure of a company whose yogurt was acceptable for Nova Scotian consumers but not for anyone who lives beyond the provincial borders, she went on to say:

The government doesn't care that the Joneses have made exceptionally delicious, high quality, entirely safe yogurt for 26 years... (It) doesn't care that 43 people depended on Peninsula Farm for employment. It doesn't care that the pasteurization method used at Peninsula Farm was working well. It doesn't care that the yogurt in the plant when the inspectors closed it was a quality product, or that dumping it was a wanton waste of good food.

This "government way, or no way" approach may be the simple way, but hardly the best way. It provides a single solution to a problem, not necessarily the best solution, nor the only solution, nor the cheapest or most efficient solution under all conditions and circumstances.

One wonders if that one acceptable solution is chosen, not because anybody believes it's best, but because it requires no bureaucratic thought or basic understanding of the processes involved. Government inspectors need only enough intelligence to decide whether a specific solution is being followed, yet the government grants them the power to destroy businesses without appeal or leniency. No one bothers thinking, no one considers the owners, employees, product quality, product history, or community impact. It's a black and white exercise – the government way, or no way.

Well, federal government inspectors went too far this time. Instead of encouraging the entrepreneurial spirit and rewarding ingenuity, our free and democratic government prefers its inspectors to destroy any small business that can't follow big business regulations.

It's stupid to expect all businesses to meet the same lofty regulations, despite their size or circumstances. The government must trust Canadians with some degree of flexibility, even in food safety regulations, and exchange its zero-tolerance mind-set for a more supple, common sense approach.

I could just imagine the response the CFIA inspectors might have made to the opinions expressed in the two articles quoted above. "But tell us something, Mr. Moore," they would have said in dulcet tones, "and you too, Ms. Hennigar. Would either of *you* be willing to take full responsibility for anything that might happen to the people of Nova Scotia as a result of any possible future problem with Peninsula Farm yogurt?"

I once had the experience of dealing with an inspector who would have been the answer to Marg Hennigar's prayers. His name was Vern Green, and he was the food safety inspector for my district when I was first making yogurt in my kitchen. The results were greatly appreciated in a local health food store. The product had attracted the attention not only of satisfied customers, but of a distinctly unhappy competitor as well. This man had decided to call the Health Department to complain that we were making yogurt in the cattle barn.

Poor Mr. Green arrived at the farm that very afternoon in what I could only describe as a carefully subdued dither. He clearly had something on his mind, judging from his furrowed brow and constantly working jaw muscles, but the man was calm, polite, and delicate in his approach to the question of whether manure was one of the active ingredients in my yogurt. He even managed to smile once or twice during the interview, in spite of the tense mandible.

When I showed him around the barn he was relieved to see that there wasn't any indication of a yogurt-making set-up. The cows stared at him over their haunches, wondering what the unscheduled visit was all about. The pigs rushed over to their trough and looked up at us expectantly, hoping that it had at last occurred to me that pigs are always more than willing to dispose of an extra snack at any time of the day. A desultory visit to the loft revealed nothing more than two rows of neatly stacked bales of hay, and a mother cat comfortably ensconced with her kittens in some loose straw in the middle aisle.

"This is truly a cottage industry," said a visibly relieved Mr. Green. "The kind they used to have in my mother's day."

He had gone over everything in my kitchen with a fine-toothed comb and had pronounced it clean as a whistle, to use his very words. I sat him down at the kitchen table with Valerie next to him in her highchair, and served them both some fresh strawberry yogurt.

"This here," he said, placing the contents of his spoon between his now fully-relaxed lips, "is what I call a delicious dairy product of the sort you can't find any more these days. It's too bad, too. This is the way food *should* be made – on a small scale, with pots and pans you can scrub yourself so you can see they're clean with your own eyes. But the big dairies, they have much more of a potential problem. They have so many pipes running every which way with elbows and other nooks and crannies that could easily be contaminated without anyone even knowing it. You turn the wrong valve and you've got clean-up water or something worse running through the lines. Anything can happen in those huge plants."

Where are the Mr. Greens when you need them?

CHAPTER TWENTY

Words of Reassurance

Do we smell a smoking gun?

I woke up early one morning and lay in bed wondering for the millionth time if I could have done something to prevent this calamity.

"I still can't decide," I said to my recumbent husband, "whether the inspectors were just doing their jobs and following the regulations exactly as they were written, or if they really did have some hidden agenda, as we were saying the other morning. I don't want to make the mistake of looking for conspiracies where they don't exist, but do you think there really was something behind it?

"They knew what they were doing, all right."

"How can you be sure?"

"I could see it by their attitude the minute they walked through the doorway."

"But that doesn't *prove* anything."

"Well, how about this, then? When the CFIA first started writing to me, I noticed that there was a cc. at the bottom of the page showing they'd sent a copy of their letter to one of our competitors."

"What! You never told me that!"

"I know. I just didn't want to put a bee in your bonnet. I needed you to think your way through all the stuff that had to be done right away."

"Did you complain to the CFIA about it?"

"Yes. I called them right away and demanded to know why they were sending copies of our private correspondence to our competitor."

"And what did they say?"

"They insisted that it was just a mistake, a clerical error or something like that, and the copy had never been sent out."

"Yeah, I bet. How can a clerk just decide to send a copy of some private business correspondence to our competitors by mistake? That smells like a smoking gun to me!"

"Maybe, maybe not. It could be that the inspectors showed up at their plant and gave them a whole list of expensive changes to make, and the plant manager got mad and said if *they* were going to have to make changes, then the inspectors better hustle on down the road to Peninsula Farm and make sure *we* made the same changes, too, or it wouldn't be fair."

"I don't know about that."

"Well, you know how kids are. You send one to bed early, and the first thing she says is that her sister has to go to bed early then, too."

"But the CFIA was going to come here anyway. We ship product across provincial borders, so the competitors knew we were on the list. So why would the inspectors feel obligated to send those people a copy of their letter to us, proving to them that they were going to inspect our plant, too? Why would it be any of their business? It sure sounds to me as though they were communicating pretty closely with the competition about things they had no business knowing."

"I don't know. You could be right. Or maybe they just wanted us to go to bed early."

"Yes, but the inspectors didn't feel the need to assure *us* that they had inspected *their* plant. How do we know they weren't in cahoots? Don't you think it's possible that those competitors *sent* them to find something wrong?"

"I wouldn't want to touch that one with a ten foot pole," said Gordon. "Not unless I had proof."

"I'm not accusing anyone. I'm just asking questions. I'm allowed to ask questions, aren't I?"

"Yes, but don't point any fingers."

"You told me yourself that the inspectors seemed to have an agenda right from the beginning. They rode onto the farm like bunch of cowboys."

"That's true. I had the feeling that they knew in advance that they were going to give us a hard time. On the other hand, maybe they're like that with everyone. But we're not that cozy with our competitors, so there's really no way to find out."

The bee in my bonnet was starting to buzz. I decided to use the Freedom of Information Act to apply for the CFIA's correspondence concerning our case.

As soon as I finished breakfast I got on the phone and called Denis Châtelain, Analyst for Access to Information and Privacy at the CFIA in Nepean, Ontario, and asked him to send me the file on the pre-registration inspection for Peninsula Farm. Although I felt a bit awkward about having to ask the Canadian Food Inspection Agency itself to help me in carrying out my fact-finding mission, Mr. Châtelain was polite and accommodating about my request. He told me he'd send me the file the very next day.

When the file arrived I was amazed to see that the CFIA's correspondence concerning their inspection of our plant that day was several hundred pages long. Good grief! What are we paying these civil servants to *do* with their time?

After settling down at the kitchen table with a hot cup of coffee, I noticed something that I found rather curious. On one occasion Brian Ward wrote a memo to one of his fellow inspectors asking her to prepare herself very carefully for their inspection of the Peninsula Farm plant, as it could go *political*. How did they know in advance that they were going to do something that would end up creating a public outcry? A normal inspection does not go political. We had been inspected countless times in the past (every week, in fact), and there was never any reason for any of the inspections to come to the attention of anyone outside the purview of the interested parties. So why now? Why on this specific occasion?

Another item that interested me was the fact that the CFIA admitted that they had tested the yogurt that was already on the shelves *and could find nothing wrong with it*, even though they had tried their best to uncover something they could complain about. And this was *before* the inspection, too! So they were actually *trying* to find reasons ahead of time to find fault with Peninsula Farm's factory and/or manufacturing processes. This bit of information was proof positive.

As I continued to read on, I came across yet another piece of telling information. The inspectors had contacted their lab in Ottawa, asking them to analyze our previous test results and to compare them with tests performed on yogurt sold in Ontario. A lab tech wrote back and told the inspectors that the yogurt on shelves in Ontario stores received lower scores on their test results than ours did. She didn't think there was any reason for them to be concerned about our product.

So how did the inspectors react to this reassuring news from their own specialist? They simply ignored it.

It was hard for me to believe that the federal inspectors weren't trying as hard as they could to find fault with a yogurt that, according to all sources, was the best available on the market. Why on earth would our public servants want to commit such a cruel and destructive act? Did it feel good to see what they could do with their power? Did our government employees have the same mentality as common vandals? Charles Moore certainly made a good case for it in his article. Be that as it may, whatever their motive, I felt it behooved Gordon and me to do our best to see that it never happened again to anyone else.

As for the copy of our private correspondence that had been sent to our competitor – the action that had motivated my search of the CFIA's files in the first place – I found nothing further on this subject. It was hard for me to believe, however, that it was only a clerical error. How could a secretary or a clerk mistakenly send a copy of a letter dealing with the inspection of our plant to one of our competitors? I could only hope that the mystery would be solved some day. But so far I haven't uncovered anything new.

Storm troopers

Once again, the voice of the people of Nova Scotia made itself clear on the subject of what should be done about the injustices meted out by our elected government officials.

Shame on the bureaucrats who have shut down Peninsula Farm, wrote Pat Parker of Northwest Cove, in her letter to the editor of the Bridgewater Bulletin. *It is time we demand that the power we bestow on politicians come with accountability. We ask for reasonable measures of safety and we receive endless rules, a maze of red tape and civil servants with taxpayer paid solicitors.*

We must remember that we are the government and if apathy is the problem, then only we can change that. They say, "you get the government you deserve." I believe it should be, "you will get the government you demand."

C. Bailey, in his letter to the same newspaper, expressed similar opinions:

Everyone seems outraged, but is any action being taken or will the whole affair fade with our anger after a few weeks? So frequently I hear words like, "Well, what can you do, it's the government?" But if we all remain so gutless, we are giving over our power to a dictatorship. Like Gandhi's civil disobedience, or Walesa's Solidarity Movement, the will of the people eventually overcame injustice.

"Maybe we *are* just gutless wonders," I said to Gordon, after reading Bailey's comments. "Maybe we should have tried harder to be heroes, like Gandhi or Walesa. The inspectors got away with it, and we couldn't do anything about it! Maybe we should have fomented a revolution, or something."

"Canadians aren't ready yet for that sort of thing," Gordon replied. "Revolutions only work in countries where the people are in despair. I don't think we've quite reached that point yet."

"But that's the whole idea! Citizens should make sure their countries never do reach the point of despair. That's why I wish we could do something now, before it gets worse."

"Well, I think we've already done everything we can. We've contacted every politician short of Jean Chrétien, and I'm not sure what good that would have done, anyway. We have no money to start up again, and we're too old to borrow money and expect to get anything back on the investment. There's not enough time left in our lives to be taking financial risks. Our employees don't have the wherewithal to buy the business, and venture capitalists aren't going to want to build a new factory when the business would only be able to support a limited number of consumers. A factory like that belongs in Quebec or Ontario, where the bulk of the population lives. So I don't think you should beat yourself up about it."

"I guess you're right," I sighed. "But it never should have happened in the first place. And I don't want to see it happen again, to some other poor sucker."

A letter to *The Chronicle-Herald* from Walter H. Leslie of Pictou said it all:

A month or so ago, every politician in Nova Scotia was gleefully slamming Alliance Leader Stephen Harper over his so-called derogatory remarks towards Nova Scotians (i.e. that we need hand-outs from Ottawa because we can't take care of ourselves). *Now, they have a chance to put their money where their mouths are…*

Ottawa sent in its storm troopers from the Canadian Food Inspection Agency and shut down a Lunenburg company called Peninsula Farm. This was a small Nova Scotian business which exactly fit the bill for every Tory, Liberal or

*NDP candidate who ever ran in an election in Nova Scotia:
"If we are elected, we will do everything in our power to
promote and protect small business."*

This is exactly the scenario to which Stephen Harper was
referring. *Small business in the Maritimes has no protection.
This company was shut down without prior testing of its
products by people who did not even know how to do the test.*

John Hamm (the premier of Nova Scotia) *should use the
notwithstanding clause in our Constitution to override this
federal decision, and Darrell Dexter and Danny Graham*
(politicians from the other two parties) *should back him to the
hilt. Money should be found to help Peninsula Farm and put
it back in business before it's too late.*

*Stephen Harper is right. If "they" want it, they take it.
Nova Scotians don't have the population to stop them. Coal,
fish, lumber, farms, gas stations, anything to do with rural
Nova Scotia is being destroyed by civil servants and big
business.*

Back in the early stages of the fiasco we asked John
Hamm's government to grant us the money to put us back on
our feet again. His representatives listened politely, but were
only willing to consider *lending* us the necessary funds.
Gordon and I were left with the impression that they believed
that if a small company can't "compete," then it shouldn't be
propped up with taxpayers' money. Not one of the people at
the meeting was willing to admit that it was the federal
government itself that had crippled us and made us unable to
"compete" in the first place. *If "they" want it, they take it.
Rural Nova Scotia is being destroyed by civil servants and big
business.*

Not everybody was of the opinion that we were not fit
enough to survive. John MacDonnell, MLA for Hants East,
wrote an excellent article for *The Sunday Daily News* about
the failure of the Tory government to catch the ball.

*The Joneses would like to see Peninsula Farm continue to
be a success story in the hands of their employees,* he wrote.

This would take some help from the provincial government –
about $1 million, most of which would go to the building of a
new facility. I don't believe Nova Scotians would see this as a
bad investment, in view of Peninsula Farm's track record and
its large, supportive customer base.

As the province has already given a $3-million tax break
to Sobeys, a $27-million write-off to Michelin, and, more
recently, the restructuring of debt of $8.5 million owed the
provincial government by Pure Energy Battery Incorporated,
Peninsula Farm seems a pretty safe bet.

How often have we heard the same story? The
government can readily find millions of dollars to shore up
large companies, which it considers to be a "safer" investment.
But significant sums of money have also been lost on these so-
called safe bets. Many of these giant conglomerates are
headquartered off shore (like our competitors Yoplait, Groupe
Danone, and Parmalat), and they can close down local
branches whenever the spirit moves, causing the loss of untold
numbers of jobs. It's much safer, it seems to me, to bet on a
hundred local small businesses than to throw money at one
multinational whose interest in the local economy is likely to
be slim.

Take the case of Parmalat, for example. This giant food
corporation is located in Parma, Italy, which is well known for
its Parmesan cheese. The company has been a transnational
conglomerate for many years now, buying up smaller
businesses in countries around the world. In the late 90s it
gobbled up Astro, a medium-sized dairy in Toronto, and then
proceeded to do everything possible to dominate the market in
Canada, including, of course, right here in our own back yard.

So far, so good. That's the way business works in today's
society. Astro, in fact, had considered buying us before they
were acquired by Parmalat, perhaps so they could hand them
our share of the Maritime market as part of the deal. It's bad
enough when large corporations force smaller ones out of
business. That's competition, and free enterprise has its cruel
side. The situation is worse, however, when the multinationals

acquire so much power that they can dictate terms and decide the future of less-developed countries and have-not provinces. But the worst case scenario is when huge corporations like Enron, for example, not only wreak destruction but leave everyone holding the bag.

That is exactly what Parmalat did. Once the pride of the region's milk and dairy industry, the corporation grew so powerful that it got too big for its boots. As so often happens in cases like this, certain executives milked the company dry and then blithely declared bankruptcy. When this occurs on a grand scale, people sit up and take notice, especially the ones who are left holding the empty milk pail. This is what *The New York Times* had to say about the situation on February 15, 2004:

The Italian minister of industry, Antonio Marzano, said yesterday that he would meet with Italian banks within 10 days to form a committee to represent creditors of Parmalat, the publicly-traded dairy company, during bankruptcy proceedings.

Italian banks, Italian bondholders and foreign creditors will be invited to take part in the committee to give them a role in the reorganization of Italy's biggest food company and a say in how its new management tries to pay off $17.8 billion in debt, Mr. Marzano said.

Parmalat filed for bankruptcy on Dec. 24 after disclosing that a $4.9 billion account at Bank of America did not exist. The company sold more than 80 percent of its $10.2 billion in outstanding bonds to American investors, and there are also 75,000 holders of Parmalat bonds in Italy.

That's right. Parmalat's $4.9 *billion* account at Bank of America *did not even exist!* Why, one might ask, does our government like to deal with corporations that have the power to pull off a coup of this magnitude? Maybe it's tempting to do business with a giant corporation that offers to create a few jobs, lowering the cost of goods and services through greater economies of scale, and sweetening the deal in the process by lining the pockets of the facilitators.

Multinational giants provide the comfort of quick solutions to the ever-gnawing problems of budget deficits, unemployment figures, and re-election. They seem like a safe bet because we assume that huge companies are run by financial wizards who know what they're doing, and who'll never get us into trouble. But when a fiasco does occur, the results can be disastrous; and it only takes one to wreak economic havoc.

A risky business, indeed. It would be a lot safer to have a solid economic infrastructure made up of local businesses. But when you invite a Trojan horse into the city, there's a price to pay. I would hate to see Canada become a nation of grooms.

CHAPTER TWENTY-ONE

Caveat Patria

Killed by friendly fire

I s small business going the way of the dodo? We protect endangered species in the natural world, and it only makes sense for us to consider doing so in the economic world, as well. Nobody accuses ecologists of protectionism. We all understand the importance of protecting the balance of nature, so it shouldn't be very hard to make the connection with the global economy, which also needs to have its balance corrected once in a while. Giant corporations are growing like weeds, and they are choking out some of the valuable plants that contribute to our general health and well-being. What sort of a world will it be when they finally succeed?

Marge Dahn of Centre, Lunenburg County, has this to say in her letter to the editor of *The Progress Enterprise:*

What has happened to Peninsula Farm is a tragedy. For over 25 years they have made wonderful yogurt, the best on the market, striving over the years to compete with ever-increasing multinational corporation incursions. Since NAFTA (the North American Free Trade Agreement), *they have seen American and European companies fill up greater and greater shelf space in the grocery stores.*

Citing their pasteurization process as a reason for closing is a red-herring. Their method is superior to the one the Canadian Food Inspection Agency requires. Provincial inspections have never found anything amiss. Their product has been respected and loved by thousands of Maritimers.

I believe this is an excellent example of the incursion of multinational corporations on local business. Their influence in Ottawa is disproportionate and often contrary to the public good. Under the General Agreement on Trade in Services (GATS), this situation will only get worse. More and more multinationals will provide products and services which previously local businesses have provided while bringing good livings and healthy products to us all. Profits from multinationals leave the province, depleting our community's well-being. Enough is enough.

Big business is on the march. Globalization has already damaged the economies of many a less-developed country whose small businesses have been ruined by the cheap products produced by multinational corporations. One often hears the argument that the people in those countries benefit from the availability of cheap products, but when their own businesses die in the process, the economic infrastructure is often damaged beyond repair. What happens to democracy and the right of the people to govern themselves and make their own decisions? One can't help wondering who elected these giant corporations to the throne of power.

Globalization and the empowerment of large corporations is leading in many new and strange directions these days, not the least of which is the genetic modification of our foodstuffs. Nobody knows as yet what, if any, effect the changes may have on our health, but I'm concerned that corporations are patenting DNA sequences, which gives them legal ownership of certain new strains of fruits and vegetables. Not only is it dangerous to meddle with the genetic variation that has taken centuries or even millennia to develop, but the privatization of genetic material is questionable in so many ways that it would take an entire book, or a library of books, to do justice to the subject.

Meanwhile, the poor are starving. Many agencies and even large corporations are making generous contributions in an effort to stamp out sickness and poverty, but it's really only a finger in the dike. We see the same problem in nature all the time: once the environment is destroyed, the animals die. In the same way, when the economic infrastructure of a poor country is destroyed, human beings pay the ultimate price. Now we are beginning to see the deleterious side of globalization in our own countries, too. Giant corporations are putting small local companies out of business, and their employees are losing their jobs. The same corporations are outsourcing many of their own jobs in order to keep costs down, but this only leads to even more unemployment. There is a good deal of talk about creating new jobs by retraining the unemployed, but that could be another finger in the dike. The jury is still out on the results of this effort – one can only hope that there are sufficient new jobs in the future to offset the ones that are being lost every day. Meanwhile, the federal government continues to favor big business and harass or close down small businesses.

Here is what John MacDonell, in his article to *The Sunday Daily News,* has to say on the subject:

It is obvious from census data that rural Nova Scotia is losing people. The Chignecto Central Regional School Board recently announced about 30 lost teaching jobs in the Pictou and Cumberland areas because there are not enough students. Keeping schools open, attracting doctors, and economic development are related issues. Governments have a role to play. Keeping people working is the first step in securing the sustainability of a community.

The Joneses (built) their small, kitchen operation into a $2 million-a-year business, with 43 employees. The then-Department of Agriculture and Marketing promoted Peninsula Farm as the success story it was.

So what happened? Why has the Agriculture and Fisheries Department been unable to broker any compromise with its federal counterpart? Why has the Economic Development Department not entered the fray? If another entrepreneur now were to come forward with a proposal to produce a value-added product from a raw material and create 40-plus jobs in rural Nova Scotia, what support could they expect?

Isn't the success of Peninsula Farm the success story that governments, politicians, entrepreneurs and communities dream about? Isn't a success like this what we still need in Nova Scotia?

One might well ask. As Walter H. Leslie points out in his letter to the editor of *The Chronicle-Herald*, rural enterprises such as coal, fish, lumber, farms, and other small businesses are being stamped out by big business and their putative allies, the civil servants who work for big government. For big business and big government are indeed, as Andy Rooney said in his TV interview, in bed with each other. It may be warm and cozy for them under the blankets, but it makes no sense for a government to kill its own small corporate citizens with friendly fire. The irony is that the governments themselves will pay the ultimate price, for when you share your bed with Goliath, you'll feel pretty uncomfortable when he rolls over on you.

Womb Raiders

Anyone starting a small business knows that after all the years of sacrifice and hard work it becomes a part of the family. It's even more – it becomes your baby, a sibling to your other kids.

So you can imagine how I felt when I got a letter from my lawyer saying that some anonymous party was petitioning the Trademarks office to acquire the trade name "Peninsula Farm." Some opportunistic person or organization had decided that since we had gone out of business, he could just take our name and all the good will that went along with it, and appropriate it for his own unmerited benefit. The name of this raider was protected by client privilege, we were told.

"Yes," I thought bitterly, "we certainly want to hide and protect the name of any wanton raider who is too immoral, too greedy, or too cowardly to contact us with a proposal to buy our company rather than steal our name."

I realize that there has to be a system for recycling unused trademarks, but it must surely be outside the intention of the trademark rules for some random corporation to consciously go out and use a name just because it may have some continuing benefit to that individual or company. It's particularly galling when such an entity has accomplished nothing whatsoever to merit the benefits acquired from the name. I felt as if someone were trying to steal my child, and the police were aiding the kidnapper. How was this any different from someone taking the identity of a dead person before the body was cold in the ground, in order to cash in on the reputation of the deceased?

The company representing the interloper was a prestigious, expensive law firm in Toronto, which leads me to believe the raider is a corporate wise guy rather than an individual. Could this opportunist be the one behind the visit from the inspectors? We will probably never know until the Frankenstein version of Peninsula Farm is created by the shadowy would-be raider pretending his organization or his company is actually the real thing. I can't wait to see the final act of this ongoing drama, when the identity of the villain is finally revealed.

Daisy and Goliath

"I still feel blue," I said to Gordon one morning as we stood at our front door surveying the devastation. "I don't think I'll ever feel better until I find a way to make sure this whole mess doesn't happen again to other small businesses. I just can't bear the injustice of it all. It's not right. It's not fair. I just *hate* it!"

Gordon put his arm around my shoulder. "If one person could fix it alone, the world wouldn't need an ark," he said.

"We do need an ark, but nobody's listening, and nobody's building one, either. Some day we're going to have to rescue the animals, two by two, and all the people as well."

"So just keep on writing your book. Maybe some day it will become a rallying call to other folks out there."

"I don't know that much about economics, though. I don't have the right vocabulary to express those concepts, either."

"It's all jargon, anyway," Gordon said. "I think you'd be doing the world a favor by just writing the story of Daisy in a perfectly straightforward way. There's nothing wrong with farm vocabulary, since most everything is BS anyway."

"Get away," I said, taking a swipe at him.

"Use it as a tool to talk about the dangers of globalization when it runs amuck. I'm not saying there's anything wrong with sensible economies of scale. Of course there's a place for big business in the world today. But when greed takes over, that's something else. It's a form of fanaticism. The fanaticism of greed is what leads to corruption and injustice. So go to it, girl. Show them how a cow took on the big boys. It's about time they grappled with an animal they can't control or even understand, for that matter."

"That's right. Remember how you tried to get Daisy into the barn after she had her first calf out in the field? She paid no attention to you. You pulled on her halter, but she refused to go with you to the barn. She wouldn't follow you at all. She just went right on grazing."

"I remember," said Gordon. "Then Travis Oickle came along and scooped up the calf and carried it to the barn, and Daisy trotted right along behind him."

"Travis was a lot wiser than the puffed-up CEOs who run the multinationals. They don't usually put the people's interests first, do they? Remember the day when the pigs escaped and we couldn't round them up and get them back to their pen? Along came Travis with a bucket of pig feed, and they all followed him to the pen as though he were the Pied Piper."

"Exactly. Pigs rule! Cows, too. Our little farm is a microcosm of the outside world. When people read your story, they'll see the connections right away. It's a good case study. Just tell it the way it happened. Make Daisy stand for something. But don't use ponderous language from the economics textbooks. That would only kill it for the readers."

"My grandmother used to say, 'Isn't it funny? Bees make honey. Men come along and think it's money.'"

"There you go. We interfere with everything that's natural and good as we traipse around in our big clodhoppers looking for the pot of gold. Bulls in a china shop, that's what we are. We're the most destructive species on earth. But it doesn't have to be that way. We have an eye for beauty, and an ear for poetry, and a heart that yearns for goodness and mercy."

"May they follow you all the days of your life," I smiled.

We stood there looking out over the sparkling ocean. We felt sad that our days on the farm were numbered, but we knew we didn't really own the land we had tilled for so many years any more than we owned the ocean that lapped its shores. There would be other oceans and other shores, and we would watch the waves breaking in their usual way, in the pattern familiar to people from the beginning of our days on earth, long before the human race aspired to own the natural world.

As I gazed at the beauty around me, I felt honored that Gordon and I had been entrusted with those twenty-five acres for twenty-five years. I felt happy, too, that we had provided so many people with yogurt made from the milk that Daisy had so generously shared with us. She was the epitome of unruffled magnanimity. If there is a heaven for barnyard creatures, she will surely be in it. Her meadow will be forever fresh and luscious, it will smell of timothy, clover, and chlorophyll, and it will never be subject to the inspection of earthly bureaucrats.

What will become of Goliath, that great nemesis of Daisy the Cow? We didn't bring him down with our slingshot. As far as I can tell, the fall of Peninsula Farm did nothing to stop Goliath in his tracks. That ungainly troglodyte is still marching forward, his lumbering stride making the very earth tremble. But sometimes giants are vanquished in unexpected ways. It must have seemed unlikely to Joshua that the walls of Jericho would fall at the sound of trumpets.

We can raise our voices too, and point to the giant who is gobbling up the fruit of our labor. Goliath is not as powerful as he looks. He will fall some day of his own weight, knocked flat by the last stone from the last catapult.

And Daisy will prevail, a beautiful brown cow, grazing on the green, green grass.

Epilogue

Many people have asked why Sonia called this book *Daisy and Goliath*. In the biblical story David slays Goliath, the metaphor for the might-makes-right corporations and governments of the world, whereas in our story Goliath ends up killing Daisy. Some agents and publishers refused Sonia's manuscript on the grounds that the ending of the story is not only a downer, but it doesn't even come close to following the biblical story for which it was named. I can only say that the story of Daisy and Goliath is just beginning to take shape in the world, and we haven't seen the ending yet. But Daisy, meanwhile, is a perfect symbol for the peaceful, hard-working folks who are trying to make ends meet in spite of the looming shadow of Goliath, who is already wreaking havoc on the business, political, and social fabric of the world community.

Our pastor, David Vroege, told me that if I were to write an epilogue for *Daisy and Goliath* as I wrote the foreword for *It All Began with Daisy,* it would be like bookends for the Peninsula Farm story. This seemed to us to have just the right touch, so this outburst from the usually silent partner is my contribution. Unfortunately it has taken me a long time to get over my anger at the injustice described in Sonia's tale. In fact, I still occasionally flail around and sputter when I think about it, but I've calmed down a lot since then.

People have asked why we didn't sue the government for behaving in such an unfair manner. Believe me, we waded into this battle with our eyes glowing like coals, but the prospect of drowning in our own bile was not very appealing, and the costs were prohibitive from a risk/reward standpoint. We did speak to a prestigious lawyer who agreed to consider our plight on a contingency fee basis, but in the end the law and the precedents caused us to abandon the idea of seeking justice from the very government that had created the travesty in the first place. Because I was seventy-two at the time of the closure, we knew I didn't have much earning-power left in me, so I wouldn't be able to seek retribution in an amount large enough to make it worthwhile to file a law suit. I'm sure there was also an unspoken assumption that the government lawyers would stall long enough for me to croak before a settlement would be made. The government has unlimited funds – yours and mine – to use in its defense, and this irony did not escape us either.

You may think they got the better of us, and so did I for a period of time. For years I had been clinging to the yogurt vats by my fingernails. We had been swimming against the tide, expending great efforts, but not moving ahead. Our business had become our lives, and we seemed to have no future. I developed a healthy new empathy for Sisyphus and his endless travails.

So being forced to let go of the yogurt vats turned out to be a form of divine intervention, and far more of a reward than a death sentence. I began to view the glass as half full, and when I did that, it ran over. Sonia and I still had each other, after all, and although our retirement was not going to be as financially carefree as we had hoped, we were getting by. When we finally began to look ahead instead of behind, we crossed the Rubicon. Defeat turned into victory. We were irrevocably committed to the present, to the future, and to each other.

What of the future? Well, so far it has been marvelous, a descriptive word I never would have used to picture our lives during and after our closure. But we have found the time now to plumb each other's depths, and to our great surprise we've discovered that there is more to life than what can be found inside a vat of yogurt. We have been blessed with good health, and the habit of working hard persists even into our dotage. In addition to this book, Sonia has several other writing projects in the works, and even I have managed to write two novels of questionable distinction. Our daughters, whose pictures were on the back cover of *It All Began with Daisy,* are grown, married, and educated (a physician and a teacher), and we have even broken through the grandparent barrier.

To those inspectors, competitors, and other ill wishers, we can only say we forgive you, and we hope that by now you have grown well beyond the point of only doing your jobs.

Gordon Jones

Final Word

Wives always have to have the last word, so bear with me for a moment. I couldn't end this book without mentioning Travis Oickle, the name I gave to our next door neighbor. Those of you who read *It All Began With Daisy* will remember that he was invaluable to us in the early years, as he taught Gordon how to milk cows, make fence, and repair all kinds of arcane machinery (including the ever mysterious wall switcher). In return we lent him our brand new farm equipment for plowing and making hay. He thought this was the best deal in the world, and so did we.

One morning, shortly after *It All Began With Daisy* was published, Travis came to me and told me that a friend had read the book and said it was some good.

"But why did you call me *Travis Oickle?*" he wanted to know. "That's not my name. You oughta know that!"

"I was trying to protect your privacy."

"I don't have no privacy."

His wife Marion looked up from her knitting, frowned, and went back to the ribbing she was working on.

"Well, I didn't want any tourists to come knocking on your door, asking you questions and wasting your time."

"I got all kindsa time. Gordon don't need me no more, so I don't have that much to do."

"I could think of some things," Marion said.

"I'm sorry," I said. "I had no idea."

"Well, if you ever write another book with me in it, I want you to use my real name. Gibbie Rhuland."

"Your real name is Gilbert," Marion reminded him.

"Nobody calls me that."

"Well they should. You're not a little boy."

"Will you do that?" he asked me. "Gibbie Rhuland. Don't forget. I want my friends to know I'm in a book. I want to be remembered. And don't forget, I'm still waiting for that wall switcher."

"I haven't forgotten. I promise I'll waltz with you the very next time the Lunenburg Volunteer Fire Department has a fund-raiser."

"Don't hold your breath," Marion said. "Gilbert's got two left feet."

I never did have that waltz with Gibbie. He died of cancer before the next fund-raiser. But Gordon and I will always be grateful for his companionship and his wise counsel about farming. The name of Gilbert Rhuland, inscribed herewith in the present book, will long be remembered. So will the name of his older brother, Ernest Rhuland, who was the talented foreman for the construction of the *Bluenose II*, and who made me a model of the original *Bluenose* schooner that I'll always cherish. The name of Gibbie's other brother, Arthur Rhuland, will also live on, for his wife, Joan Rhuland, was the sister of Peninsula Farm's own Cheryl Lohnes in accounts receivable.

One day Gibbie asked me to talk to the folks at Michelin to see if they would hire his son, Terry Rhuland. I did, and they did. He worked there for many years, until poor health forced him to take early retirement. So the name of our good neighbor Gilbert Rhuland and all the other Rhuland names will live on, thanks to a Jersey cow named Daisy, who made it all begin.

Sonia Jones

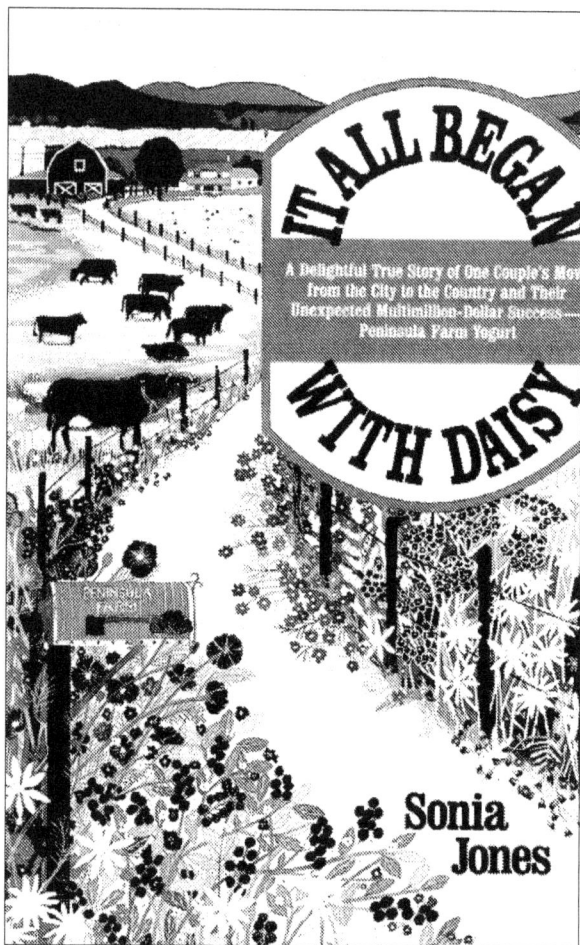

It All Began With Daisy
A Delightful True Story of One Couple's Move from the City to the Country and Their Unexpected Multimillion-Dollar Success—Peninsula Farm Yogurt

Sonia Jones

If you enjoyed reading *Daisy and Goliath,* you will also like the prequel, *It All Began With Daisy* (Dutton/Penguin, New York, 1987). You can get a brand new hardcover first edition at www.erserandpond.com, or you may send a check/money order for $25.95 (please add $2.16 for sales tax plus $8.00 for postage and handling) to Erser and Pond Ltd, 1096 Queen St, Suite 225, Halifax, Nova Scotia B3H 2R9, Canada. Checks and money orders should be made out to Erser and Pond Ltd.

If you would like a personal autograph by Sonia Jones, please indicate the name of the person to whom the book should be inscribed.

Editorial Reviews

Bob Coleman, New York Times
Some stories have inherent charm... To describe her unusual achievements, the author has constructed a breezy, well-paced narrative, with nice descriptions of the Canadian countryside and cheerful character sketches of her neighbors and business allies. Inverting the conventions of business autobiography, she describes her blunders - both technical and in matters of human relations - with a pleasing comic style. Indeed, the best things in It *All Began With Daisy* are its author's good humor and genuine charity of spirit. . . .

The most appealing idea in her book: the notion that small-scale capitalism can help preserve both ecological balance and individual freedom. Especially when applied to farming, the vision brings out the Jeffersonian in us all; and the author is always cheerily optimistic about its prospects, as when she describes the tourists who visited the farm each summer: "The chickens would fatten themselves on maggots, slugs, and various garden pests; the pigs would take care of the wastage emanating from the kitchen or the dairy-case shelves. . . . Finally, the tourists would liquidate the farm-related food products so that the cash could then be used to keep the business growing, thus completing the circle." It's a striking passage - a sort of yuppie version of Virgil's "Georgics," with a notable element of truth. . . .

Mrs. Jones has a born teacher's eye for the well-chosen example. Her book's succession of quick incidents neatly conveys the rush of challenges, disasters and successes, of emotional highs and lows, which makes being an entrepreneur so exciting and - for some of us - so addictive.

Jim Morrison, Publishers Weekly
The eponymous Daisy is a cow that the author and her husband bought when they moved from New York City to a farm in Nova Scotia. Daisy's yield of milk proved to be so plentiful that the author was able to make yogurt for local store owners to sell. As the fame of the product spread so did its sales, and the business continues to reward the husband-and-wife partnership. The author relates the story in an engaging fashion, even describing setbacks cheerfully. There is added charm in accounts of veteran farmers whose advice was invaluable to the couple, to whom rural life at first was utterly alien.

Marilyn Linton, Lifestyle Editor, Toronto Sunday Sun
What's especially interesting about Jones' story is that her company became a success in spite of itself. It was in business before it even had a name, it had no plan and no start-up money. That's nothing short of amazing when you consider that everything written or said on entrepreneurship stresses developing a solid business proposal, having a sound marketing plan and spending a small fortune to launch the enterprise.

Pauline Carey, Toronto Globe and Mail
The inevitable growth of the house the Joneses built is funny, but there is a more telling side to the story of these small entrepreneurs. Starting with sound bees in their bonnets about quality and honesty, they had to deal constantly with the strange logic of bureaucrats and the curious customs of bigger businesses such as supermarket chains. They appear to have hung in there with astonishing and unceasing good humor.

Kathryn Falk, Nonfiction Reviews
This is the inspirational book to read when you know the grass is greener on the other side of the subway fence and you want to get out of the rat race... the Joneses are now celebrities thanks to their high-quality products and their funny and heart-warming story. For an old-fashioned, delightful experience,

read this true-life romp of two urban professionals let loose on a farm.

Jennifer Henderson, Toronto Financial Post
A colorful parade of well-drawn characters and comic-tragic events - from a leaky filling machine to three years of production built upon a kitchen stove and Canadian Tire Styrofoam coolers - all but ensures the Jones' life will soon be the subject of a made-for-TV movie. (Would Jane Fonda consider playing the confident and unstoppable Sonia?) Other cast members include Travis, the laconic neighbor who offers homespun advice on everything from plumbing to bovine psychology; David Sobey, the fairy godfather who "discovers" Peninsula Farm and invites the Joneses into the Sobey supermarket chain; Yvette, a French-Canadian dynamo who regales her health food customers with equal portions of spoonerisms and sensual descriptions of strawberry yogurt; and Eddie Shoemaker (Fast Eddie?), the grasping chain store buyer who teaches Sonia the hard, cold facts of the food industry... "When it comes to business," muses Sonia Jones, "small is terrifying, but medium is beautiful." The Yogurt Queen has arrived.

Amazon.com
★★★★★ **Captivating Story** Aug 15, 2007

When I first read this engaging book by Sonia Jones in 2002, I couldn't put this book down. Closing the last page, I attempted to look up Peninsula Farm, envisioning a trip to Nova Scotia, only to find the farm was recently shut down. Appears the farm continued operating well after the book was published.

★★★★★ **An inspiring book filled with humour, local colour and charm** Apr 16, 1998

It All Began With Daisy is an inspiring book filled with humour, local colour, and excellent storytelling. It is encouraging to read the adventures of such an entrepeneurial couple and their "vigorous muddling" through the years of establishing their yoghurt company. Characters come alive and conversations quiver with the skill of the author's recounting. Highly recommended for light, inspirational reading.

www.ingramcontent.com/pod-product-compliance
Lightning Source LLC
Chambersburg PA
CBHW070952040426
42443CB00007B/471